Timeless Advice

Timeless Advice

… just like in the old days!

MICHAEL ZIBRUN

ARCHWAY
PUBLISHING

Archway Publishing books may be ordered through booksellers or by contacting:

Archway Publishing
1663 Liberty Drive
Bloomington, IN 47403
www.archwaypublishing.com
1 (888) 242-5904

ISBN: 978-1-4808-5448-2 (sc)
ISBN: 978-1-4808-5449-9 (e)

Library of Congress Control Number: 2017917595

Print information available on the last page.

Archway Publishing rev. date: 12/11/2017

Contents

Foreword

*"**Timeless Advice**", just like the old days!*

Hello! I'm Mike Zibrun, author of *Timeless Advice*. For years, now, I've been writing a small weekly column to help folks like you and me, stay <u>positive</u> - *in a goofy world that seems to be spinnin' like a top.* My template, if you will, was and is my Polish-Slovenian heritage, and my wife Carols' passionate Italian roots. I will forever remember on holidays how we talked around the massive dining room table, everyone with opinions, passion and humor ... and everyone reverting to the language of the street and not the textbook.

My inspiration in writing fell to two folks I continue to admire for their wit and unpredictability. *Mike Royco* – Page 3 guru of the Chicago Sun Times Newspaper -painted sweet stories in 500 words or less, and *William Sydney Porter*, or *O'Henry* to most all of us, and was a master wielder of "words" whose endings were always a surprise twist.

Our large family meals around our dinner tables were legendary, in their profuseness of opinions, curious word choices in more than one language, malaprops and a passion to always be in three conversations, simultaneously. (Those of you with big families get it.) So, gentle reader, just sending you some good old fashioned family advice your way. Have fun, experience maybe a flashback or two of your own, and let the language flow.

Dedication

That this book is even written, is testament to the love, generosity and patience of my late, sweet wife Carol, and the support of our Children Mike, and Jenny and daughter-in-law Michele who often critiqued the columns, or found themselves the subject of same. I'm indebted to good friends – true friends who were my *august body of Critics* and who were encouraged to slash freely in insuring the writings had currency. Of course, all of the columns are faith- based and without the spiritual Guidance and inspiration of God, this book wouldn't exist. I'm simply the messenger, I mean, He did invent the words, **after all**!

I hope you find yourself touched by a column or two, or maybe even grab a lifeline, yerself, to get *you* through one of lifes' *tough* patches. Oh, and don't forget to smile! Always smile. He likes it when you smile.

...Hey! Your *A-A-A* Coverage Has Been Renewed!...

My friends, don't you have great Peace of Mind when you get insurance protection against the unexpected? Isn't it comforting to be able to turn over a difficult situation to someone who will be there to get you through it? Well, today's *good news* is that you've had that coverage ... <u>Since you were born!</u>

Of course, this protection isn't a claims policy, it's a *beneficiary statement*. It's designed specifically for you when you find yourself and those you love in difficult circumstances. It is simply how you turn to God in times of testing and trial, for yourself or others who are in your prayers. The application form is easy to complete.

There are three parts to the form:

Authenticity: When you ask God for help, ask from your heart and your soul and not for benefit, but for relief.

Acceptance: Surrender to Gods' answer to your prayer. Accept His way and will, which you surely do not know, His way and will, be done. God answers prayers in various hidden ways...ways we need not see.

Appreciation: Thank God for hearing your prayers, in humility and love.

Authenticity, Acceptance, and Appreciation...your **A-A-A** coverage, 24/7/365.

..."Choice" is more than just a grade of meat...

Ya know, we got a pretty good gift from God when He was creating us at the beginning. Everything from mobility to dexterity, brains for our heads, and hearts to be shaped and molded, and we got free will for our intellect and humility for our spiritual nourishment. Yeah, these are all pretty good things to have, cause without 'em, well, it's not pretty. Oh, and I almost forgot, He also gave us the power to decide things. **Choice.**

Ya see, Choice is a powerful and wonderful gift for good—or a horrible and faithless act for evil. Choice allows us control over our destiny, and that can be good when choice involves God's plan for us. We are free to fashion whatever forms for ourselves we wish to be. But we also have the choice to degenerate into the lowest forms of life. So here's a few thoughts, this day, on perusin' "yer choosin'"....

Choose to love, not to hate.

Choose to laugh, not to cry.

Choose to create, not to destroy.

Choose to persevere, not to quit.

Choose to praise, not to gossip.

Choose to heal, rather than to wound.

Choose to give, not to steal.

Michael Zibrun

Choose to act, rather than to find an excuse for inaction.

Choose to pray, rather than to curse.

Choose to live, rather than to die.

You are always determining your own nature in accordance with your Free Will. You were made in the image and likeness of God. But we need to constantly ask ourselves whether He is well pleased with the person you or I have become? So, wadda ya think? If yer not wildly enthusiastic about yer answer, well, *just choose differently*, that's all! Great things happen -His Plan for us, with good choices!

...Mercy, Mercy, Mercy...

Hey, Time Machine here! Going back to Friday Nights at Loyola University, Chicago Illinois. Dance Mixers on the North Side of Chicago, September, 1967, *the place to be for the best Chicago bands.* In particular, one great group called The Buckinghams, who just happened to be playing their new hit that night, "<u>*Mercy, Mercy, Mercy.*</u>" *That song would be destined to hit #5 on the Billboard Charts.* But, before they added their lyrics, "<u>Mercy, Mercy, Mercy</u>" was debuted by the Cannonball Adderley Quintet in 1966, with a *whole other slant to it.*

The Cannonball Adderly Quintet was ***the*** group in 1966. Cannonball actually gave props to his Piano man, Joe Slawinul, for the words to the music. He was fond of telling the story that... ***"We think we're ready to handle anything, and the world kinda closes in on that kinda thinking, and when the bad times roll, we're caught short, ya know? Sometimes the only thing you can think to do, because that was how yerr mommy and daddy brought you up, is to just ask for mercy."*** Amen to that, eh?

Folks, ya just don't know when some gentle nudge and inspiration from the next life will come along and kinda nudge its way into yer conscience. A lot o' times, folks just kinda brush it aside like hair in yer eyes. But once in a while - especially if yer hittin' a rough patch -ya just might pause ever so slightly and run those thoughts around in yer mind. Nothin' happens by accident, and what happens next is maybe when the song begins to sing to others. Check out the Buckinghams on the web, and Cannonball's version too! Mercy me!

Michael Zibrun

...Is There Something on Your Mind Today?...

Ya know, sometimes I wonder if the descendants of Ringling Brothers and Barnum and Bailey aren't scratchin' their heads about the world all around us? Hey, this is almost too big to talk about in a small book. But, We've gotcher animal acts over in Ring number one, the elephants and the donkeys, and the clowns are spraying each other between the first and second ring. The third ring is going to the dogs, and between the rings… we've got yer guy getting shot out o'the cannon while the princess is holdin' on by her teeth to the rope of peril. The second ring of common sense and decency and moral values is strangely empty amidst all the chaos, noise and whipped cream.

Ah, there come the monkeys … always the most interesting act in town. Ya know, folks monkeying with this or chattering around with that. They usually stay out'a sight, but on rare occasions where there is a banana to steal or a back to scratch, they're front row center.

What is a ringmaster to do? Well, the show must go on, and that's understandable, but then its' sure gotten outa hand when the acts begin to take over the show. Ya see, the show was never supposed to be taken over by the acts. Yet through history, folks of dubious purpose or background have always been there to try and hog the glory or to take the power or the image. The Ringmaster has given 'em a lot of latitude to make sure the show goes on, but when the third-rate acts act as if they are they're the star attractions, it's no wonder everybody is slippin' on the banana peels.

So what's a body to do? Well, I don't know about you, but I'm tempted to take a broom and cart to it all and do what I know in my soul the Ringmaster wants me to do, make good choices and help clean up the acts. He wishes you and I have the ears to hear and the wisdom to ignore the insanity and *get on with the show* because the show ain't passin' back this way again till the Big Top is ready to fold its tents, as the tour ends and the memories drift away like old smoke.

Michael Zibrun

...Ya Wondering if God Even Knows yer Alive Today?...

Well, since the world was formed, God deemed that Bazillions of folks should occupy this big blue marble, and by golly, here you are too...a Bazillion and one. What makes you so special that God shines His light on you, Mr. or Mrs. or Mz Bazillion Plus One? Do ya think God really cares about you amidst the countless Bazillions before ya? Well, what do the scribes say about you, oh one of a Bazllion?

Well, Psalm 23 says this:

THE LORD IS MY SALVATION
Hmm … amidst the countless souls, He singles you out.
HE MAKETH ME TO LIE DOWN IN GREEN PASTURES
Hmm...He knows that through rest your strength is built up, so enjoy it!
HE LEADETH ME BESIDE STILL WATERS
Hmm...He knows you also need a quiet time in order to seek balance.
HE LEADETH ME IN THE PATH OF RIGHTOUSNESS
Hmm... He cares enough to hold your hand and make sure, of your steps.
FOR HIS NAME SAKE
Hmm...He has had a purpose for YOU since before time began.
YEA THAT I WALK THROUGH THE VALLEY OF THE SHADOW OF DEATH
Hmm... He loves you so much, that He trusts you to trust in Him.
I WILL FEAR NO EVIL
Hmm...He extends His protection to you.
FOR THOU ARE WITH ME
Hmm... Your Faith in Him sets you free to reside in Him.
THY ROD AND THY STAFF, THEY COMFORT ME

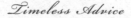

Hmm…You are protected, watched over, and safe.

THOU PREPAREST A TABLE BEFORE ME, IN THE PRESENCE OF MINE ENEMIES

Hmm… He has always had a plan for you, regardless of where you are in your plans

THOU ANNOINTETH MY HEAD WITH OIL

Hmm… He consecrates you with protection

MY CUP RUNNETH OVER

Hmm… His simple abundance is unending.

SURE GOODNESS AND MERCY SHALL FOLLOW ME, ALL THE DAYS OF MY LIFE

Hmm… He blesses you in ways unknown from His endless font of Grace.

AND I WILL DWELL IN THE HOUSE OF THE LORD

Hmm… He desires to have you choose His way, not Yours.

FOREVER. (1)

Hey, He never releases His Hand from yours. Don't you let go either, ya hear?

All this … for you.

...When Prayer doesn't come easy...

We might be surprised to know how much of a prayer life we really may _not_ have in today's world of information overload. And that's just the reality of the world we live in. Suffice it to say, there almost seems to be a conspiracy to make sure that there is no free time between thoughts, or even some time to "mentally coast" for a bit. Last time I checked, the world is still spinning at about the same speed as it did eons ago when God set the whole shebang in motion. However, the invasion of our private spaces, our measured thoughts, and our quiet reasoning seems to be working toward Mach 1.

It's sure tough to have a healthy and virtuous prayer life when we're already told there aren't enough hours in the day. Even Ferris Bueller said that "the world moves pretty fast." And, it's pretty sad when we fall into the trap of just accepting, that ... that's just the way it is ... _'cause it don't have to be that way._ That's a choice, not an inevitability.

You can take back control of your prayer life, any time you want. You just need to say ..."_enough already._" I think we've been conditioned to feel obligated to always be "in noise." Yet, any time you want, you can cancel that contract and say _enough, already_! **But why would we want to leave all that excitement behind?** Because in truth, we really do cherish, the quiet ... the time to decompress ... the chance to appreciate those moment when we can just "be". Those are often the times when we allow that gentle breeze from God to actually be felt ... or the beauty of one of His sunsets, the sound of children's laughter, the quiet spiritual moment that _just came outa nowhere_ ... the chance to say "Hi" to the One who never, ever stops thinking of you – lest you would disappear if He ever did ... stop ... thinking of you. Remember, He said *"Before you were formed in the womb I knew you"* (2). So how about your thinking, seeing, feeling Him today, in everything **you** do ... and thank HIM, that He created you to also be able to pray to Him.

Michael Zibrun

...Gods' Promises In 26 Letters
Of The Alphabet...

"*A*lthough things are not perfect, *B*ecause of trials or pains, *C*ontinue in thanksgiving and *D*o not begin to blame ... *E*ven when times are hard, *F*ierce winds are bound to blow, *G*od is forever, able. *H*old on to what you know, *I*magine life without His love ... *J*oy would cease to be, so *K*eep thanking Him for all the things *L*ove imparts to thee, and *M*ove out of "camp complaining", for *N*o weapon that is known, *O*n earth can yield the power of Love. *P*raise can do it alone. *Q*uit Looking at the future and *R*edeem the time at hand.

*S*tart each day with worship, for to *T*hank is a command, *U*ntil we see Him coming *V*ictorious in the sky ... well, *W*e'll run the race with gratitude, *X*alting God on high, and *Y*es there'll be some good and yes some bad times too, but *Z*ion waits in glory,

Where none are ever sad.

So just remember that the shortest distance to a problem, is the distance between your knees and the floor, and the one who kneels to the Lord can stand up to anything.

... Don't forget to say "thank you" ...

We need to remember those souls who've taken time in their lives to pray for us. And that reality kinda triggers a question for us to _ponder_ ... *When was the last time you said "Thanks!" to all the people who have prayed for you in your life?* All Souls is *–after all-* past, present and future.

Think about it ... while you were in yer mom's womb, there were prayers being lifted up for you ... when you were born, or were sick, or were facing the challenges of childhood, boundaries, facing tests, or trying to sort out school and life relationships, folks were there, *praying for you.* In your later life, with work, family, adult relationships, marriage, children ... maybe even grandkids, the stresses of making bills, braces, birthdays, times of testing and trial with family or illness ... and a thousand other things. There were people who were praying for you. How many tens of thousands of prayers, or *hundreds of thousands –or more - prayers* were lifted up **just for you** in your life?

UH ... like who? Like Prayer groups you'll never know about *in this life* ... Prayer cards to religious orders who pray for you daily, friends, strangers, Mass intentions, general intercessions, classroom prayers, and much, much more. Wanna almost touch Heaven? Listen to a 4 year old pray, for you. Through your whole life, people have been praying for you, as well as *all souls*. **So?**. So, don't forget to do, what our Mom said we should do ... say *Thank you!* to all the kind souls who prayed for you ... by *your prayers back* to them. And, pay it forward, friend. Pay it forward.

...Redemption ...

We've all experienced in life that moment ... when some real bad thing happens to some good person. Often times, it's that proverbial "bolt out the blue" that no one saw coming. And it has consequences. Most often we think of this with health issues, but it can just as easily be about family dynamics, money issues, Faith crises or sudden new responsibilities. Where's the answer book or the example of how you deal with all that?

"Heavy Burden, Heavy Load", as Tess use'ta sing. Yet one is not alone, ever. Jesus walks with us just as He walked for us. And His walk was to redeem us for our salvation. There are those who try to look at their "cross" through the eyes of Jesus. Those who come to view their burden as Redemptive Suffering. Past the shock, they accept their burden, this, never expected heavy load, and endure that new and frightful walk with their offering up of their pain or suffering for others, ...of self ... who have it worse than they do. The seventh Station of the Cross recounts the suffering Jesus endured for our sins- "by His stripes, we were healed.(3)"

How we look at these tests of Faith or Tests of Life, is our choice. But in the lesson of Jesus on His way to Calvary, we may find example of offering our test and trial as Jesus did. _For others_. God doesn't plan for bad things to happen, it's just life and choices. How we react to the trials on our journey of life by enduring the burden for another who may have it worse, is the example Jesus left for us. One is never alone, never forgotten. His strength, dwelling in us on our walk, accepted for another ... gives that walk purpose and that journey, redemptive. This is your great, nobility.

...When my 'Mapquest' had the folds' ... scotch-taped...

Once upon a time, before the advent of no-filtered, say anything with no consequences "media" or apps, *Civil* Conversation was done through face-to-face. The phone was merely the vehicle to set up the place of conversation. As owner, sales rep and coffee pot cleaner in my own business, my secret weapon was a most cherished *City of Chicago Street Map*. Long before Siri, Sorry, or Sadly, I had the golden ring. Y'see in the old days not really all so long ago, and before technology overran our lives and ruined many folks' communication skills and Acceptable Boundaries, permanently, I had the best weapon ever.

Yeah, there were them maps that every gas station in the country provided, but for a 100% guarantee of getting' ya where ya wanted to go in my part o' the world, there was none better than that prized beauty mentioned above. Sure, we had our dear friend Officer Baldy, in the WGN-sponsored helicopter, who let us know accurately when bumpers conspired to tie up traffic ... *and his suggestions for getting around the delay caused.* And that was good to know, but I had the Holy Grail ... and its' invitation to bypass accidents or construction sang its' siren song to me ... flawlessly.

I actually still have it, in case the Smithsonian calls and wants to put it on display in an exhibit of twentieth century *"tools of the sales trade"* Exhibit.

I treasured my copy, remembering the old adage that if ya don't know where yer goin, any road'll take ya there. And, almost always, my route plan to get to a prospective client was flawless. Well, like me, it's got a lot of fold lines and wear and tear, and a piece missin, here and there,

Michael Zibrun

but through all the years, it never let me down. Hey, - *he sez, tying this all together* - when was the last time you picked up a Bible and just read, some? Do you have your own Favorite "Road Map?" ... maybe Wisdom?. How about Isaiah? Luke?

If'n ya don't, go back to "old dependable" ... The truly one and only Good Book – just like I used to do in the secular world, and follow the directions – including the side streets when appropriate ... even over the verbal creases that might not quite line up properly ... Cause once ya got the right tool to get ya where ya wanna be, you can count on it to deliver you to where the Mapmaker knew he'd want ya to arrive at. Safely at your place of destination ... *cause the Bible tells you so.*

… And now for something completely different … courtesy o' yers truly…

A prayer, for most always …

Lord, soften my heart,
Ease my anxiety,
Help me with my burdens,
Most of all, help me with my stubbornness
I'm a work in progress,
Sometimes I'm **really** a piece o'work
Sometimes I get more minuses than plusses
And more often than not,
I set the land-speed record for bad choices
But, I do love you, Lord
I really do
And I know you put stuff in front of me,
And sometimes I just keep walking past
But I love you Lord, Help me to be humble
Help me to turn around
'cause that's the only way I can really wake up
… and really mean it…
I surrender. Use me as you see fit
And I really do want to make this work right
That's your work, for me, to help
But I can't do it without you
That's the reality of Life
You gave me that, from Day 1
Use me, Lord, as you see fit

Michael Zibrun

...Peace, Brothers And Sisters ... Blessed Peace!...

Now there is a *thought* that bears looking at closer in this goof-nuts world we live in, doesn't it? But sometimes, the older we get, the more it seems like an abstract concept. We get a lotta stuf pullin' and tuggin' at us ... the clock seems to speed up and the stuff cryin' fer immediate attention steals our energy, our rational thought, and derails our natural desire for order. Don't believe me? Watch the tube for 30 seconds and see how many times we're moved to a state of anxiety (unless yer watchin Happy Days!)

When the Lord separated the land and the water(4), back at the beginning, Peace was the way God planned for it to be. And, sadly for us, that Plan for us, "died, a'borning" when disobedience got rationalized with entitlement. (That means "I want what I want, and I want Yours' too." And life, well, it was never really the same, after that.

Y'see we crave the one thing we really desire, Peace ... and are immediately buried under an avalanche of free will choices we make to insure we don't have it. *That is – on our own terms.* Games o'chance ain't a solution. Yet PEACE *IS,* what God makes available to us, always! We just sorta get in our own way sometimes, or the evil one throws everything including the kitchen sink at us to get us to lose heart. **_Don't._** God didn't go away, you are not alone, you are loved unconditionally because you are a child of God. Y'know the song *"Let there be peace on Earth, and let it begin with me"* is a pretty good instruction from top management. Your free choice also includes choosing God's way for you. So here's the instruction manual summary: Let Go, Let God ... and don't ever let go of His hand, ... ever.

"…And the song, goes on …"

Earlier in life, I used to teach that if one could completely commit to something, simply to be 1% better at it - and really, really mean it … that would always result in 3% more "good end results." Y'see, Ya always get more than what ya put into it … it's like getting Green Stamps after a good choice. (ask yer grampa) And so, look back on the good works and good sacrifices you made for others. Oh, you may not always be able to see the results of your good works, but that's OK. That's why we call it Faith. You just have to do to do it. What if the gifts and graces and intentions you received or others benefitted from, were allowed to continue, even multiply in good ways?

Think of the good you've done for folks you cared for, and wanted to help with prayers. You'll never know of the power of those prayers for others, in this life, but that's OK. It's not about keeping a running total, it's about doing the heavy lifting in support through prayers. Pleasing God by your selfless action, is always reward enough.

And yet, Maybe - just maybe - you get back something, in mysterious ways, much more than you'll ever realize from your willing sacrifices and good works. The other "Good News" is that there is no expiration date on the gifts you've offered and on the grace you received.

Imagine what great work and internal Peace of Soul would result from making sacrifices now your life long practice? Imagine the good works and grace you can continue to give by really, changing nothing, but continuing your offerings of prayers? How much is a 3% return on your 1% "investment" for the rest of your life? As the music tells us …"*and the song goes on.*"

Michael Zibrun

... Somewhere in Time, and Eternity ...

Back in the day, me and the missus (*she who will be obeyed*) my sweetie Carol, were groupies! -Nah, not like at Radio guy Steve Dahl's disco destruction night debacle at Chicago's Comiskey Park in the old days, but rather, "regulars" fer a bunch o' years at the Grand Hotel, on Mackinac Island ... "tween the two Michigans. Y'see we saw a movie called **Somewhere in Time** on early 80's cable and fell in love, with the love story. We'd go up each year and hobnob with the cast, crew and new friends and kinda "live" in that era fer a couple o' days in late October, after all the "day-fudgies" went home at the end of the tourist season. Even got to pal around with some of the swells, like Paul, Sue, Bill, Richard, John and a touch of Christopher.

Well, the Story Line actually came from a Well Known Science Fiction writer Richard Matheson, who attended several of the events. Richard had a solid reputation in Hollywood and several of his movies scripts, like **Somewhere in Time**, made it to the big screen. Interestingly, his arguably biggest hit was a script for a movie called **The Incredible Shrinking Man** (about just that happening). His Prose elevated the genre to sublime elegance. So I told you that, so I could tell ya this. His story ended with a haunting soliloquy voiced by actor Robert Scott Carey (the shrinkee), in the films' final moments.

Y'all probably saw the movie, and if ya were like me, y'all probably never expected such true poetry at the moment of Robert Scott Carey's character. I mean, here he is, facing oblivion ... and he's not rail'n against God, his lot in life, all his plans fer the future, now shot, tattered and blown away. So instead of cursing fate, he turns away from worldly reactions, and contemplates his onrushing fate. But not onrushing, toward oblivion, but rather as a page turned in his eternal life to come. And he crosses that barrier of regret over to the reality of eternity ... and realizes that while he may be the smallest of the small, he will still exist, because there is no Zero. He does not die, he still means something. And by extension, so too, do you, gentle reader –no matter what life may throw at you, to try to reduce you, to nothingness,

But don't take my word for it, check out how the Author of that story, and that character put into prose, a most elegant realization of the Eternal. Check out Richard Matheson on the web and search for his written soliloquy for Robert Scott Card.

Hero Worship isn't 4th Row Center Aisle

We don't seem to talk much about Heroes anymore do we? I can't recall the fancy Awards Shows mentioning **that** category for recognition, but they sure seemed to throw out a lot of *"who really cares?"* platitudes. Y'see, I think we as a people kinda got lost here on who should be getting the attention and recognition for best performance in an ongoing life.

Let's see. I think if I remember this right, ... *should God stop thinking of anyone of us for the smallest fraction of a moment, we'd cease to exist. And then there's ... There's no trial that you face in life that God can't help you through ...* And of course in the category of Redemption, *we are all called to be redeemable by our good works, our prayers and our example to others, without counting the cost.* We may not recall who won Best Actor, but a month from now God will have thought of you, <u>individually</u>, around 2,764,800 seconds – roughly – but continuously. How've you returned the favor?

Y'see, we seem to take things like air, water, alarm clocks and chocolate for granted ... *always have, always will.* But, not really. The only constant in life is God, and that ... is upon whom your eyes, and your heart, gentle reader, and your connection and your eternal future rests. **Everything else,** everything is small stuf. There is no best seat in the house, every seat is the best seat. So if ya wanna worship a HERO, how about the one who created you? And the one who has invited you to spend eternity with HIM? THERE is where your treasure lies ... *for all eternity. May we ALL get it right,* brothers and sisters ... *<u>get it right</u>.*

...The Art of Advertising, or the Greed of goofballs?...

Having spent pretty much a whole lifetime in the disciplines of Advertising and of Communication, I felt ever so nominally qualified to comment on the *"persuasive disciplines"* I'd made a career of, in earlier times. In my formative years – culminating with **Finally! g r a d u a t i n g** from college - I set my sights on what I believed was an honorable profession, that of "Advertising and Marketing." To me, and the good folks who honorably made up that profession in those earlier days, there was much currency in honest and effective communication about *"why consider A, over B?"* if ya get my drift. There were standards, and values, and boundaries back in the early days, and occasional abuses, but generally values were based on the good that came from the objects of attention, all our human condition. But, to me, that landscape was pristine and that craft, I believed, was generally practiced with values, ethics and morality. To me, ah … *the age of innocence.*

Today, remembering my craft of long ago, I witness screaming headlines, fast talkers slamming 100 words of terms/conditions into 15 seconds - to meet a legal mandate on their product or service- a remarkable lack of depth about feature, function, value. And, most sadly, a departure from the high ground of storytelling and subtle selling, to a default of mass transit messages. Blah blah blah blah! Scream and Arrogance are the new norm. Believing is so hard, sometimes. Bullying is, so easy, much of the time. Ok, so who's the source for my well rounded observations? Well, nothin' like the Good Book to give us the secrets of that craft. What a place to turn to! Yet most any and all values you or I have in life, come from that Operators' Manual called the Bible. In there, you find values espoused, examples

Michael Zibrun

illuminated, absolutes shared in ten thousand different ways ... Mercy portrayed as almost another Beatitude, and ... Comparisons and Consequences if bad choices seem enticing, and, overarching all ... the Warranty – Who and What stands behind the Promise. And, best news ever, it's written on most any of the pages in simple language ... the Promise. I'm eternally grateful the Lord steered me like He did, and that He guided me so that I tried to make life not about ego, but tryin' ta get out His Message ... while, occasionally flopping sensationally!. But, I try, to not lose sight of The Truth, The Promise., And in eternity, *the Warranty.*

…Helplessness means … do more!…

Those of us with receding sun-bleached blond hair, or maybe no hair, sometimes look back in conversation, about the times, maybe we ran outa gas, and a stranger helped, or makin' the bills was rough and kind relatives like Jeannie and Frank, or friends bailed us out. Or, maybe life dealt us a rotten hand, and some kind souls got us through the rough patches. Truth be told, if I could remember, most anything at all of those "friend in need" moments of the past, I think I'd amaze myself at how many many times folks were there, who chose to … be there for me and the missus … in our helplessness moments.

Y'know, we read in our church paper about needin' folks to help out for lots a' good causes, or we read in the news about the need for volunteers for good worthwhile help when disaster hits, or hear on the tube about a need for food donations, or maybe, every so often just another set o' arms and legs to help others. I don't know, maybe we just can't add another thing to our plate. But when we try to remember those who came to our aid, when we needed help – back in the day - or maybe even last week when the outflow exceed the income … and somebody just like you or me stepped forward to help, and didn't need a "thank you" – it was just the right thing to do. Y'see, helplessness means someone saying "Lord, I'm outa options." Saying *Yes* to that momentary need, changes black into white.

So maybe when them God moments to help come along and ya feel a tap on the shoulder from on high, maybe it's time to pay it forward. Maybe it's time to just say YES. Maybe it's time to do more, than you had planned - and give back to those in rough waters or howlin' winds … or to help a cause, or to pray for someone or to just do a good thing. Maybe that's the plan He had for you and me from the beginning. So, here goes … Here I am, Lord …

Michael Zibrun

... When Plan B fails, miserably ...

There is no setback in life, really, that God doesn't have a *comeback plan for* ...

Someone once asked God ..."*If everything is written in destiny, then why should we wish for something?*" Well, what kind of a question is that? Did you just fall off the turnip truck? Cheese Louise! Does that mean we don't have free will to choose our own course, our own destiny, our own plans and dreams and desires and our own place in history? Y'know, we're kinda busy here, and the world is yellin at us ... **this is your time, this is your life, what You believe- You will achieve!** ...

Y'see, things happen fer a reason, and mostly, we're all often kinda blind in lookin' for that reason ... while we "seek to carve out our place in the history books, social circles, group status, or the lead dog in our admiration society." That might be in our families, network of friends or in broader recognition and admiration from the media or business circles. Clip and save it! ... *Refrigerator Art-Recognition from our peers, eh?*

Nah. What did Jesus say to the Apostles, swampin' in the boat? ..."*keep calm, and praise Him, in the storm.*"(5) That's it! Amid chaos, smell the Roses! Faith always trumps fear. In the world, some are becoming so needy of validation and sympathy that they fail to realize that what they have, is what they deserve. So, reach out! **Hey, when it's too hard to stand, kneel!** In that genuineness, there is where we find our trust in God's way and will. After all, when we asked God what we selfishly wanted to wish for ..., did we not realize that God sometimes answers us "*Maybe in a few places I have written, As you wish.*"

... and now, Refrigerator inspiration for the hungry soul ...

I've heard it said that the collective "whew"! exhaled after we got past the secular nonsense of the holidays (not Holy Days) actually sped up the world by 3 minutes. So like the deflated characters which we may have had on our front porches or yards, we slow our pace, and get back in balance again. Thank Heaven for the signs, wonders and Faith Practices to ground us well, against the stormy distractions, eh?

So, in that spirit, here are a few one liners, that may brighten your day with Peace ...

*"There are at least 15 people in the world
who love you in some way"*

"Every night, someone thinks of you, before they go to sleep"

"You mean the world, to someone"

"Always remember that you are truly God's gift to others"

*"Friends are Angels who lift us to our feet
when our wings have trouble"*

*"In all humanity, from the beginning to its
end, there is only one, of you"*

"God don't make no junk, no how, no way, ... never"

"He loves you, every single second of your life."

"Your prayers have great, great power."

<u>Now, just believe it.</u>

...Dance, I hope you dance ...

Hey there, Time Machine again. This time it's 2000 AD. A crossover country singer by the name of Lee Ann Womack had two great, great friends in Mark Sanders and Tia Sillers who gave her a true gem of a song for the ages. It so simply laid out the path of faith to follow, in everyday life.

She sings of the innumerable times of prayers, wishes and dreams hidden beneath our breath ... and of what it takes to Hope... and Hope takes never ceasing to be amazed, that you matter, that you make a difference.

... so Breathe in, and soak it up, you hopeless romantics! There's countless grains of sand beneath you, innumerable ocean waves before you and yet while you are small, you are irreplaceable.

So when you swear in spite of your weaknesses, to struggle through, you do a beautiful thing. Courage is all about surrendering to He who gave you courage. In the beginning.

Trust is nothing more than saying ... OK. It is in the dance, that joy, renewed hope, openness and trust thrive. God didn't give you two left feet, he gave us one left and on right ... DANCE! You hopeless unromantics may not get it at first, ... *but you will!!!*

That record soared to #1 on the Billboard Country Charts and was in the top 15 of all time county, and #1 Contemporary Charts too. Hey, don't take my word for it, check out Lee Ann Womack on U-TUBE, and savor the elegance of the words by Mark Sanders and Tia Sillers ... and the second time you play it, **DANCE!**

Michael Zibrun

... Regret is now the number 1 distraction word in our vocabulary ...

Yup, all the analysis is completed, results have been tabulated and votes have been counted, as the word REGRET is now the official most overused word in the English Language. I regret to inform you of this fact, but it now takes its' place as the worst overused word we have.

Boy, oh boy, do we give that word a world class workout. It sure seems so! Now it's not that *regret* is a bad word, for regret is part of the illumination our conscience provides for decisions made or action taken (or not taken) that had a wrong consequence. You know, things like regretting something you said, regretting something you did (or didn't do), regretting your not thinking something through, even regretting a decision that made things worse. And probably tons more, too.

When it gets goofy, and you feel overwhelmed, remember, God didn't invent regrets to lay guilt trips on us, but to improve us in His image. According to the experts, REGRET actually began with some sort of fruit on a tree, which had apparently huuuuge impacts on those two decision makers who launched that popular phrase ..."*learning the hard way*". Think about it, God never intended us to dwell in "the what if's", He intended us to dwell in the what is's! We could spend an entire lifetime on the woulda, shoulda, coulda's, and miss all the best parts of what God has given us in this life, or we can bask in the grace of all best parts of what God has given us in this life. Yesterday's a cancelled check, tomorrow's a promissory note, today is golden ... invest wisely.

Live today, really live today, with no regrets.

...Last Call For Apollo 17,
Leaving Pad 39 ...

I still remember as a young man with a small family, visiting my folks down in New Port Richey, Florida, about the time Apollo 17 was in the final prep stages of getting ready for launch the next day. The Flight Command Pilot was Gene Cernan – a Bellwood, Il. boy from our old neighborhood who made good. We drove to Pad 39A the day before launch and marveled at the majesty of that sight. We all had never seen a launch live before, and were excited we'd be able to watch it rise in the night sky from Mom and Dad's home. It was scheduled 12:30 am Dec 7, 1972 – the first night launch of a manned capsule. For my wife Carol, Mike, Jen and Mom and Dad.. and myself, it was a full circle moment. We had stared up at the moon from a beach late one evening on our honeymoon in St. Thomas in 1969 when Neil put his first footprint on the Lunar soil 250,546 miles away. And here we were, ready to watch the last launch to the moon and the last footprints made, on the moon. Well heavy nighttime ground fog killed that viewing, but still a sense of history – some 45 years later, nevertheless.

What ya may not know, is that like most all of the Apollo moon shots before and including 17, it was off course 90+ % of the time. It took a constant series of slight adjustments, thruster burns or guidance correction to assure that the capsule and the Lunar Landing Site would be where the guidance thrusters and geometry placed the rendezvous, on December 11, 1972.

Y'know, we all experience those mid-course corrections in our own spiritual lives. Maybe we're off course with God's use of us, 90% of the time too! So often, events, or choices, or moments beyond our control occur that could cause us to miss grace moments, ...God's use of us,

Michael Zibrun

opportunities spontaneous, and - once in a blue moon - something where we actually see the grace of God using us for his purposes. May we be we open to those worker bee moments so that in some oh-so-small assignments we may please He who made all and is pleased when we, hit the target too.

Gene's gone now, Neil's gone too, and the few remaining Saturns are monuments. But God continues to provide those grace filled moments, of using us to benefit others, to help others hit the targets that God intended them to reach. For me, that's AOK.

..."Where have all the gov'ners gone ... long time passin'?...

New reports just in show that there has been a massive theft across the country of Gov'ners, and officials are at a loss to explain how to counter the thefts. It seems that access to various communication mediums, has usurped common sense and all of the filters and courtesies extended in social conversation and human interaction have been pilfered ... and we're suddenly victims of grand theft.

It used to be called the niceties ... proper social interaction, dialog and respectful conversations. Nowadays, rant and hijacked children's nursery rhymes have become pseudo acceptable communication mediums that has obsoleted the sage advice offered in times past ..."*Engage brain before speaking or writing.*" No matter where ya turn, whether it's in print, tweet, one upsmanship, blather or innuendo, we don't often engage in constructive give and take conversation anymore. Instead, it's all about letting yer ego go nuts so that taunts becomes the new highjacked verbal-*Palmer Method* of communicating. (ask yer mother).

I think it's time we take back the country, folks. Free speech ain't motormouth. Free speech should be intelligent communication. It almost seems that the many communication devices we have at our disposal has encouraged bad grammar, bad form, bad talking points and bad manners. Checks and balances have been replaced in large part by unchecked ego. It's time we started shuttin down this identity theft and concentrate on the civility of conversational engagement. What a thought. Intellectual conversation worth; having so that each side can explore the merits or demerits of the other, and even agree to disagree. Seems we lost that, for a bit. Let's go find it.

Michael Zibrun

...Holdin' Hands ain't just
fer the faint hearted...

To the almost hopeless unromantics …

The Dish – she who will be obeyed - use ta love to take her pre-school babies to different little destinations when the weather permitted and all the Parents' ok's were collected. They were pretty excited when the got a chance to walk over to a nearby Nursery to see the other babies (new plants) and the colors and textures.

So, like Sergeant Bilko, she'd line em up single file, with Teacher Marcy in trail and each of the precious cargos' holden hands. And away they'd march … hand in hand to the entrance. The folks there, was always glad fer the company and the chance to show off ol' Mother Nature one more time. Y'know, there's somethin' too, really special about holdin hands with yer best friend or friends. It just feels good, and safe.

So, fer you unromantic stubborn folks who decided to stop, holdin' hands in public, Wake Up! Smell the Java. Holdin' hands is the visible way o' holdin' each others' hearts. Dontcha think Jesus held Mary and Joseph's hands? As Gomer'd say, GOLLEE! We all sorta get our heads racin' with stuff to do, in six different directions that we miss the romantic moment. When ya hold hands, it's like yer sayin to the world, "check out this bond in a world gone goofy" Remember, when ya got married back in the day, yer Celebrant said *"Marriage is two people, married in Christ.* And that's a Trinity that can withstand anything the world throws at it, if ya both just hold on tight.

So, if ya kinda got away from that mushy hand-holdin 'cause it ain't dignified, WAKE UP! You hold on and Never let go. And Christs' hand will top ya both. Nothin will ever tear ya apart, if ya just all Hold Hands together. The teacher, would like that.

Michael Zibrun

...Did you ever wonder if Lips should come with a set of instructions?...

Somehow, the art of conversation seems to have been hijacked. What in past time had been known as good conversation, or banter, or a meaningful dialog seems to have disappeared ... and been replaced with throw away lines good for one insensitive laugh, a sneering dismissal, piling on responses and often arrogance to fancy up one's self as wielding a razor sharp tongue. Meaningful conversation is no longer fun, as the spontaneous combustion of the first thought of the discussion and snappy retorts, now attact all the points, and the fine art of deliberate conversation gets a flat tire.

Once, there seemed to be unwritten rules of conduct. Gentlemen or Gentlewomen once followed the unwritten rules of discourse and discouraged the use of shrillness, rudeness, indecent language and frankly the mother lode, stupidity. Much like writing, we need some sort of a verbal Palmer Method (ask a teacher) to set moral boundaries which many people do aspire to observe. *This did not include whatever transpires around the dinner table.* And, largely, the courtesies of the medium seemed to be observed and practiced.

Scouting out the "3,800" channels on my television seems to confirm all bets are off. Now, anything goes, anything is considered normal, anything that arrests yer attention is legal and anything pushing the moral boundaries is touted as the new norm. Yet, in the eye of the storm, we discover something! I think, God hoped we'd seize on this, that there is no norm but His. Family values, Faith values, Respect, Deference, Courtesies, Humility and Surrender.

The playing field has been artificially leveled by the evil one's insistence of pandering to the lowest common denominator. That's changing. Slowly, family values, folks diggin' out of otherwise evil inclinations, and just plain ol' folks weary of anything goes, are relighting the beacons of civility and decency. Will it change the world? If only one person "gets it", it's worth the effort. Remember God gave you two lips so be careful what passes between them, them, on loan from God.

...Patience is just what the Doctor ordered ...

Y'know, there must be hundreds ... gee, maybe even thousands of different ways for each of us to remember to do things we either gotta get to, or have to do because we made a promise to ... and we gotta make good on our commitment, don't we?

Stuf of the moment that we think of and have to do right away, because in 3 minutes it'll be gone from our mind. Or things we were told to do, or asked to do, or we just remembered something else we forgot to do. So we do alarms, we set up schedules. We write something down and leave the paper where we'll see it later. Or maybe we'll have a list we can scratch off, or delete. Maybe a sticky note on a coffee pot or the steering wheel, or your tooth brush.

And Heaven forbid you should forget something you overlooked, or were late on. If we're so smart, why do we go around like we're guilty of having failed to do the tasks at hand? Is that a sign that maybe our brain is too small? Or maybe we have a mental problem? Or we're not reliable? Every day, in every way, we all miss some, we all blow a task or two that should have been a no-brainer, right? *Ah, it's all bananas!* Most all of the time we're way too unforgiving of ourselves and we beat ourselves up for "failing" in our own eyes. Here's a message from God: "Knock it off!"

Hey, stop talkin' like a potato! Have patience with all things, but first, with yourself. Never confuse your mistakes with your value as a human being. We're just human.

St. Francis de Sales once said ..."*You're a perfect valuable, creative,*

worthwhile person simply because you exist. And no amount of Trials …
or of Persecutions … can ever change that! _Self-acceptance_ is the core
of a peaceful mind(6). Or as former NBC New Anchor Connie Chung
used to say about her philosophy of life … **Don't sweat the small
stuff** … and her follow up … **Everything in life, is small stuff."**
After all, Patience is a virtue, right?

Michael Zibrun

... No risk, no reward ...

Who were the greatest risk takers in all of History? Was it Adam because he thought he outfoxed God? Was it Mary because she chose to carry her Immaculate Conception? Was it Moses because he believed, and he led? Was it Joseph because he defied all conventional "wisdom" at the time and remained at Mary's side? Was it the Apostles and the countless numbers of believers who believed without ever witnessing a miracle? Or any of the countless millions or billions more to come, who. said *Yes, Lord* ... and meant it? It is said that it takes great courage to have Authentic Faith in that which we cannot touch, feel, or examine.

It take great Trust too, and surrendering to that Trust, that lets us witness our Faith, with complete certainty. And, all any of us need do, is to simply confess from the soul *I believe!!!* In my business days of old, I was fond of a quote I found that spoke to me of spirit and courage ... the courage to truly believe. It went something like this ... **On the endless sands of hesitation lie the bleached bones of countless billions, who on the eve of victory, sat down to wait ... and waiting died**(7). Let none of us ever be afraid to give up what we perceive as the "good" to for the "great." Risk taking is not a risk if the end result is a place at the table. Sure fear can paralyze, but Faith will conquer all fears.

Trust, unconditionally, no strings attached, from the depths of your soul, erasing any doubts or concerns or what if's, place your soul in His hands and confess ... *I believe, Lord. I truly believe. Use me as you see fit."* And may your resolution light the path, to your salvation.

... Hey, What's in your DNA? ...

I still have in my hot little hands of possession, that long ago Saturday Evening Post Cover by Norman Rockwell tracing the lineage of the perfect 2 car, 2 kids middle class home in a middle class neighborhood ... the perfect couple of the 50's and 60's. And, in Rockwell's perfect 50's and 60's family lineage, we discover that not all family secrets can be kept secret forever. In Rockwell's flow chart we discover that it all began with a pirate and a barmaid. No aspersions on Mr. Rockwell, but sometimes the roots of the cause (and effect) turn out to be different than what ya thought.

But what of the ones that turned our right? Turned out to be good foundation blocks? Turned out to be historical ancestors to be honored?

What if your distant, misty roots go back to a great great ancestor getting baptized in the Jordan right before Jesus? What if your hungry ancestor could have, but didn't leave, and got fed at the feeding of the 5,000? What if your ancestor fought the irritation of the extra work and cleaned up a stable a bit so the weary couple could have a place to stay that night?

Just remember when ya get down, and kinda lose heart for what's goin'on in yer life and yer wallet ... hold tight with both Hands that You are loved in ways you can't imagine, and trust, just trust, you will never, ever be forgotten by He who made all the generations – including yours! and made you in his image. Your roots go back to God. So, Rejoice! That all. *Rejoice.*

Michael Zibrun

...Making more time for screen savers in our lives ...

By any remote chance, do you happen to have tucked away in some special place, a book on "spiritual relaxation?" Or maybe yer own secret spot? You know, something or some place that affirms "hoppin' off the merry-go-round" like finding a park bench under a windblown tree to read..or just be? Yeah ... I know, you haven't had time to get to, 'cause it's a casualty of scheduling wars? Technology and Multi-tasking has taxed our mental acuity. Y'know, the human brain is a wonderful thing. It's working the moment you are born and never stops until you stand up to speak in public.

Sometimes we just need to have a periodic screen saver pop that forwards to a time out vacation. But in this case, a place that allows you to ponder the great gift that you are from God ... to everyone else. That place where you can contemplate and appreciate the great foundation blocks of your life that God has deigned you to have. ..for His work through you. Hangin' out with God ... now available at Prayer Groups, Chapels, your own little hermitage in your own place, Church, study groups and yer own conscience. Go watch a sunset tonite ... and just marvel! Peace

How about a true, real shout out to all the Motes o' the world?

Truth be told, there's a huuuge chunk of us folks since the beginning of time who will never be guilty of attaining any sort of notoriety, or notice by the world of large, by their time on this earth. Most all o' us'ns will never be captains of industry – whatever that means. Most will never be accorded any great honors, statues in the park, or any of the recognition, society deigns to bestow on special ones. Most will have spent their lives under the radar of "recognition" and simply lived their lives according to the wisdom of right and wrong.

Most will have spent their lives, providing for themselves and others. Even those who were around before the Good Book got put together, knew the difference between right and wrong, good and evil, kind acts and hurtful acts. The further back into the distant mists of history, the more likely, folks kept it simple … there were things ya did or said that were accepted, and things ya said or did that were wrong. No gray area there, no playin' with the language, no "Flip who?" Even goin' back to the Garden, there was a knowledge of right or wrong, even as the world's first cover up took place.

You and I can relate to that even in our own families today. Maybe there was an uncle or an aunt that you mocked, 'cause they didn't use the kings English properly. Maybe they didn't fit your or my image of how they should act. Maybe growing up in their own schools of hard knocks, they never learned the subtleties of polite conversation and spoke their own mind plainly. Maybe goin' back in time, they couldn't do anything but provide fer their families. And righteous people like you and me condemned them 'cause they were so easy to mock.

Michael Zibrun

After all, in terms of their contribution, they were just a mote to the eye of God. Yet, if they could return for a brief return engagement for a limited time only, what might they share about the life they led, and why they led that life. Imagine someone you may have known in your life that didn't meet your criteria … how might they respond? Well, maybe like this …

God, I am just a mote in your plan. And I have no delusions at all of my place and my lot in life. But, this I hold onto, that I am Your mote, God. And You created me and loved me, as this single Mote loved You and trusted You and did the work You placed before me, to build up your kingdom in some small way. You gave me years and health, and tests and trials and you gave me work in the vineyard too. And, in my own way, I tried to live my life, in a way, that would please you. And I tried ever so hard, to not displease you, because I can think of no worse thing in life, than hurting You. May this Mote, have acted exactly how you hoped this Mote would act. My Lord and God.

Interesting perspective, eh? May we all, get it right, folks.

…Time for another Holiday …

By Golly, Does anybody remember the last holiday we added to our calendar of reasons why not to go to work today? Well, after exhaustive research and checking with a few friends, it occurs to me, we need a new holiday. No, I'm not talking about Buttermilk days or Left handed day (hmm, I like that one) or any such nonsense. It occurs to me that we need a Peace Day.

And, while I sense a stunned momentary silence all over the world, I would suggest this one might have legs. What do we want? Peace! … when do we want it? Now!

All right, that's already been done. But the concept may have some merit. What would Peace Day, mean to you? Imagine, the world, not just your little community, backing away from most all everything, and just going on screen saver. No errands, no after school obligations for 3 different sports programs, no checklist of to do's that's longer than your tape measure, no torturous guilt because 1 in10 things got left undone. And, mostly, no shutting down of society and our crucial services during this time. Why?

Because this is your, individual Peace Day. You yourself, call the shots. You decide how you will give yourself a day that pleases you. *I know, I know*, I hear the gripes already! *"Who's gonna do it if not me? Who's gonna cover for me? Who's Stupid Idea was this, anyway?* Actually, once upon a time, we all had time to decompress a bit, play hooky, just say no, and actually cross that line in the sand, we drew. And, ya know what, we survived! Pretty cool, eh? Best of all, no one else knows. OK, so maybe it won't be the $300 spa treatment, or the best golf time on the top course in yer area. But it will be you, choosing, to step away from the riptide and be kind to yerself. Y'know God would like that too, as you are made in His image. So to, rest in His peace, on your chosen day.

Michael Zibrun

...What's in yer Future?...

Well, recent findings from folks who study such things, point to increasing attempts to collect all the moral compasses issued everyone when they were born, and replace 'em with relativism ... y'know, *it's all bananas.* Everything goes, nowadays. Or at least that's the message that's constantly assaulting us.

Ya can hardly turn on the tube or scroll through the radio buttons without runnin' into ego, violence, anything goes, nothing is sacred. Gee, even Superman and Batman hate each other. It's like being in a state of Anxiety is the new normal. And I guarantee that that was NOT what God had planned when he created the Garden of Eden ... 'cept fer that snake in the grass who didn't start out that way, but sure fell hard when he got found out. But that's what's so cool about the Faith life! When it gets goofy, we're not alone in the lifeboat! God always was, is and will be with us through the storms, the dead calm seas, the following winds and into safe harbor. It's us who get overwhelmed and unfocused by hiccup moments that scream fer attention.

So, take a look around yerself, see with new eyes all the stuf that bein' thrown at ya daily to minimize ya ... a**nd, just reject it.** Remember He walked on the water for ya, and wants you to feel, His trust, in you. Moreso, He wants ya to never let go of His hand, no matter what the outside world throws at ya. The Faith of our Fathers, the Faith of our Ancestors, the Traditions and the Teachings of our Families and the Values He put in us when we were born, all combine to level any barrier to our salvation. As long as ya hold His hand, He'll never let go of yours.

...When words, are more
than just words...

Y'know, we sure gotta lotta words in the English language. That profound statement seemed to whoosh out of me like when ya let the lips of a balloon go and it winds up on a curtain rod, or something. And, I'm just talking English words here – which don't include many of my other favorite other languages from the Poles, Slovenians and the Italians. D'yknow how many words are in Websters' Dictionary? Thought so, neither did I. So I asked Siri, my British accent cell phone, personal "Jeeves" ... and after she said "right, gov'ner ... she said it was around 600,000. Even she isn't sure.

Well, I'm not one to quibble over 10,000 words this way or that way, but I kind found it interesting that when I went thru my few textbooks from the U of I at Navy Pier in Chicago, that there are beautiful spot-on words that seem to have retired to Florida, Sun City, or the Ozarks. Great words, that implied in their meanings very precise, specific definition words ... words like *behave, embody, certainty*, and probably most all of those missing, remaining 9,997 words mentioned above.

Two words, though, literally shout out to us through the ages ... Faith ... and Trust. These are eternal for our salvation walk with Jesus to the Father. Faith. Faith is unquestioning belief in God, and in three persons in one God. Faith is certainty with no hoops to have to jump through to verify its' authenticity. Faith is **I ... do believe ...** *period*.

The man who said to Jesus, words in effect, that "I do believe in you, but first let me go and bury my father"(8) said so, in Faith that was incomplete. True Faith has no terms or conditions ... true Faith is *"Yes,*

Lord, I will follow you." For there is a second word, that seamlessly overlays True Faith ... and that is **Trust.** Complete confidence placed in one, such as you or I. Also, no terms, no conditions. And suddenly one plus one does equal three, Three, in One. And like those Fishermen who first dropped everything to walk and follow Jesus, they had Faith, and in Trust, followed Him. This is the blueprint for us to follow for our Salvation. No signs from above expected, no self arguing to talk ourselves out of, simply two bedrock building blocks to surrender to ... Faith, and Trust. One without the other, unconditionally, is tragic.

Are you ready for the coming of a King? Are you willing to put 100% into your Faith and Your Trust? For when you do, great burdens, unanswered questions, and mostly, fear, dissipate and you are left with an overwhelming peace, because you have found that Oasis you have been yearning for, *all your life.*

Sorry to interrupt … Jesus! … holding on Line 1 … His thoughts for you

"You are on an adventurous trail with **Me**. This may not be an easy time, but it is nonetheless good-full of blessings as well as struggles. Be open to learning all that **I** want to teach you as you journey through challenging terrain. And be willing let go of familiar comforts, so you can say wholeheartedly <u>**"YES"**</u> to this adventure.

I will give you everything you need to cope with the challenges you face. Don't waste energy projecting yourself into the future – trying to walk through those "not yet" times in your mind. This is a form of unbelief. **I** have unlimited resources to provide you with what you need, including a vast army of Angels at **My** beck and call.

Pray continually as you make decisions about this journey. **I** can help you make wise choices because **I** know everything – including what lies ahead on your path. Your mind makes various plans about your way, but **I** am the one who directs your steps, *if you will* … and makes them sure, and true. If you just, Trust, in **Me**!"

Ground Control to Major Tom …

Life challenges us to continually face choices, and often, to _act_ - sometimes in minor or tiny ways, or sometimes in larger, more risky ways. Now, marry that observation with the reality that many of us are also mainly **adverse** to risk (ie: *Great Idea! Outstanding! You do it!*). It is our human condition, I think, that causes us to consider the Status Quo as Safe Harbor! In other words, venture into the harbor but don't ever lose sight of land. After all, becoming **bold** is risk taking. Hmm, better to stay on Free Parking than roll the dice.

Yet Jesus *taught* the disciples to **Put out into the deep** and by extension to all of us who follow in the footsteps of the Apostles. They were no different than us, in the beginning … and yet their trust in Jesus enabled them to *risk,* and to truly push beyond themselves for the reward that comes with perseverance. Our faith requires us to be bold for bold causes … whether it's Pro Life, Abuse, Religious Freedom or Injustices.

In the sweet movie, "*The Secret Life of Walter Mitty*", there's a poignant song originally from July 1969 by David Bowie on his Space Oddity Album. The lyrics begin with the words at the top of this missive, and speak to Courage, and to going into the unknown. Our Faiths, and our responsibilities in Living those Faiths require us to also be bold and to go into the unknown, so that *light* shines in the *darkness* and His salvation message ushers in the **Dawn**. That's **our** great commission, after all.

...Hey! Don't forget to look up!...

Of all of the advice we've been given since we were little lads and lasses, the ones involving our eye directions seems to be the most consistent. When we crossed a street we were told to look to the right, and look to the left. When we came to a curb, we were told to look down so we wouldn't stumble. When we were asked to focus on a goal we were encouraged to focus the distance, y'know ... on the goal. And probably a hundred or more other instructions to help us get through life!

Yet how often do we fail to look up? We're sorta told that if ya do, yer' gonna take a "half gainer right off the curb into the arms of trouble", or miss the moment, or worst of all, get distracted. And Heaven knows, this life's hard enough as it is, without getting distracted. But for most of us, lookin' up oughta be second nature, cause most all of us have a sense that that's where Heaven is, where God is, where peace, is.

Yeah, we know that Heaven isn't a spot in the night sky like Jupiter or Venus, something you can see after dusk with a good set of binoc's or a 'scope. But it is that place that we instinctively look up for when we have a need or a desire to pray or seek God. "Lift up your hearts ... we lift them up to the Lord ... Hosanna in the "highest", He took bread into His sacred hands, and looking up to Heaven"(9) Y'see? It's ok to look around to get a "lay of the land" in this life, but it's just as important to look up ... and in doing that, everything else in God's plan for each of us in this life, falls into place. LOOK UP, and look ... out!

Michael Zibrun

...Breaking news, everyone is always redeemable ...

Remember the old saying that's been around as long as I can recall ... _three strikes and yer out!_ ...? It kinda goes along with that companion saying ... _if at first you don't succeed, try try again!._ Well, good news from Heaven in case yer experience curve has shown that yer well past the three anythings ... God's not sittin in the stands with a clip board, waitin to write ya off. But He is, waiting in the wings (so to speak) to write you in.

Y'see, we just don't seem to be able to grasp that we have a GOD who is absolute love. Bein' ordinary human beings, we sorta grade our own shot at salvation on the worlds' terms and conditions. And, if we're not careful, we could wind up thinkin' we're irredeemable and stop tryin' ... or we're hard headed – what ya see, is what ya get. And that leads to us shouting at ourselves that changin' our ways **is hopeless**, while God says there ain't no reliever in the bullpen, hang in there ... you can do it ... if you trust Me.

Self doubt, inconsolable regret, unworthiness, no leap of Faith ... are all the evil one's domain. We were not made that way, and we do not have to linger in that trap of self doubt. We are better than that. That's why He gave us a thousand at-bats. That we persevere and trust unconditionally in Him, and He will stand up with all of our countless fans who went before us and cheer mightily when we refocus on the prize ... and in each and every one of our lives ... we _all_ ... hit it out of the park!
God wins! God wins! God Wins!

... Where's your sanctuary? ...

Do you remember, or recall yer mom and dads' stories about the old days when nuclear war was not just conversation talk, but a deadly serious possibility? At Divine Infant Grade School when I was a young lad, our preferred posture, during nuclear attack training, was under our desk with hands over our heads. The fact that our class included exterior walls with ¾ of the wall glassed in, wasn't given any consideration. Later in life, I still recall with dread one Saturday morning when the chief honcho in Denver messed up the tape warnings and broadcast a real nuclear alert by mistake, and I heard the words ... **this is not a drill. Turn to while card** 5. So how would you react? Panic is the first word that came to mind. The only sanctuary my family had was a small dirt floor wine cellar in my sister-in-law Marie's farmhouse basement. Then came the _all clear_ and hearts worked overtime to get back to normal. So I told ya that, to tell ya this.

Admittedly, that's not normally how we think of Sanctuary. But, we should each, have in our homes, apartments, rentals ... whatever ... our own sanctuary spot ... a place that is a little refuge from the crazy pulls and tugs of the outside world. Only you, know best, where that place is, or should be. Maybe you already have that spot and that special time of the day, that is just for you ... not selfishly, but necessary. We all long for that _safe room_, whatever you want to call it, where everything can get back in balance again. Of course, coffee or tea with honey service is popular there, too. Y'know, when Jesus would leave to go up the mountain, or the hill, He too sought that spot where He and the Father could commune. And as He was fortified, so to may you be.

Michael Zibrun

Y'see, it's in the quiet that you and He can talk, can be at peace, can be open to the soft comforting whispers and thoughts that feed your resolve. And, that old world o' yers that seemed to be tipping over, well, it suddenly straightens up and **"flies right."**

...Hey, take a deep breath, already!...

Y'know, if you stop to take a deep breath, and try to slow down, and find the inner peace we all long for, the odds-makers at the pony track are given 3-2 odds you just might get there. Yet that light "at the end of tunnel" that gets all your vitals into the green-range again, isn't accidental. It's the culmination of what selfless acts, private prayers, spontaneous actions, or responses ya got taught by yer ma and yer pa in those long ago early years.

When you and I were younger, it wasn't so much about amassing a huge number of credits for heaven. Honestly, it was about just doing what yer heart and yer soul – and yer mom's voice in yer head, said – was *the right thing to do.* We ain't gonna know in this life what kinda smile that brought to yer moms heart muscle when she noticed it, but at right as rain, her pride in yah just went up a hundred notches … cause yah listened to good advice, and then did, good advice.

But **Wait!** It didn't dissolve away like a Selzer tablet. Your good works linger, and go before you. They always have. God loves that, y'know? They're the gifts that keep on given! Breaking news from heaven, they aint got an expiration date either. Who knows what good deed you did for someone, didn't then find that someone looking to pay it forward to another good soul in search of balance. Fer them, it's *all good! Fer you, yer ongoing* "ministry in the moment" they simply polish to a brilliant skuff-free appearance your character in life, and becomes your compass in life. You're defined by who you love, and how you love. And, God sure loves, that. Not bad, eh..fer just spreadin' the news?

Michael Zibrun

... the deadliest sentence in the world ...

Remember. When you were a little child, in times past ... maybe five, or six or seven years old? And for whatever reason, you had gone slightly astray, in word, deed and/or action?

And in that choice, you may have captured the attention of your Mom thru something that - upon reflection - was probably not one of your or my finer moments? And of course, who can forget the response of your loving mother who so sweetly told you ... _just wait until your FATHER comes home!_ This was where you or I first learned, and physically felt, the definition of the word ... **DREAD.** In my case, it conjured images of *"THE BELT."* We may quibble about length, but to my recollection I remember hearing that the belt was 5 feet, 2 inches long and dragged on the ground. It had barbs and was known to cut thru small trees on one swipe. Yet, miraculously, no matter how snarky I was ..., I don't ever recall Dad and three neighbors ever dragging it out of the garage for my perusal.

Ah, childhood. Yet, in those long ago now, days, a lesson to be learned. As we now are assaulted by the words, deeds and actions, of petulant children – sadly of all ages -who have no social or moral boundaries on what is said, or done ... in the name of attention ... one wonders what will happen when our Father "comes home?" ... when Jesus returns to take each of us to His and our Father? Yet, our *God of second chances* gives us ways to atone for past missteps, to pray for others who may be lost and need prayers for finding the path of righteousness again, and to maybe even offer prayers to help lost souls change their ways. May we look forward in anticipation, not dread, when we here those words ..."**Your Father's here.**"

... No Lives Matter ...

That's right! The "big snake in the grass" through all the centuries has its' contract renewed. Hell's newest press release, hot off the press, just announced that in light of the success in sowing fear, distrust, war, disease and evil, the NO LIVES MATTER Campaign will continue for another century – or so he sez.

That's right, based on the turmoil being created around the world these days, the option to extend the NO LIVES MATTER campaign may continue, absent miracles to the contrary. Crucial to the success of this initiative are two end results that have encouraged this move: first, no lives ever really mattered to 'old scratch' – that evil has no interest in lives – only in body counts. Secondly, given the condition of the world, the evil one shows high confidence that he's got the upper hand.

Latest breaking news from Heaven, just in, is this: **_Nice Try, get lost_**. Seems the All Lives Matter initiative, unchanged from the start, continues to bear fruit and in the midst of a world in misery and uncertainty. Top sources have shared that together, we can insure the defeat of the one who has already been removed from one office. Mother Mary has told us Catholics that Prayer, Fasting and Confession can derail for good, any fast freight train tryin' to plow through our side o' the tracks and sneak one past us, and ... we can even save the precious cargo if they realize the error of their ways, and repent.

So spread the word, in a world on fire ... that this **too** shall pass and in the end, as always, He wins ... He, our Father ... who art in Heaven. <u>Print that</u>, *hot off God's presses.*

Michael Zibrun

...“I could’a been a contender ...”...

Sometimes speaking lines from a movie have a message far beyond the script writers’ intentions. I remember hearin’ that line from Marlon Brando in movie **On The Waterfront** on cable which spoke of a boxer’s life lived in frustration at never having had the chance to get to the “top” ... frustration and disappointment at what “could’a been.” Sometimes, folks just like us sorta feel the same way. How many Golden Rings did you miss grabbin, eh? We may muse, that once upon a time, there was a plan for the future, and then fate intervened and the life led did not meet the life expected. And, we folks sorta feel bad about that.

But that simply sounds like throwing away that life, that *was*, without knowing how that real life helped or influenced the lives of others who were, instead touched. Because our lives ended up how they’ve ended up, we tend to focus on the golden ring on the Carousel we *didn’t* grab, that moment that eluded us when we didn’t cash in on a million dollar idea (like a burial quarry for Pet Rocks that died - *ask a senior citizen*), or kicking ourselves because we did put **opportunity, personal gain** before the hard, correct choices we should have had to make instead. Well, truth be told, that’s mostly Ol’ Scratch trying to get you or me to lose heart for what the evil one sez you shouldn’t ought to have lost. Y’see the more discouraged you get, the more your otherwise good works suffer.

My Carol Ann one said “what doesn’t kill ya, makes ya stronger.” To dream of the person you would have liked to have been is to waste the person you already are. And in that person you are, God has used you innumerable times for doing His good work, versus the pursuit of success – not happiness, but success – at any price. So take comfort in who you are because *as you are,* you are fulfilling God's plan. Know also that **as, you are,** you are loved, and as you act, God loves you. Y'see, it's not about being a contender, it's about allowing God to guide you to being <u>in His image.</u> Take that to the bank. God, don't pull no punches.

...Y'know, All things considered,
I'm ok with the trials ...

We sure seem to get a lot of tests in our lives, don't we? Physical challenges that 5 years ago weren't even a possibility for us to undergo ... The financial blindsides that come out of nowhere, the foundation of our good lives, crumbling a bit, the incessant screaming at us to worry, fear, or despair. It so often overwhelms the good and grace filled moments we also experience, which, God gives us to weather the storm.

But y'know what? ... of all the blessings that come from being a believer in Christ, one of the greatest is that of have an *eternal perspective* and knowing in our souls that God is always there for us, and His presence is always **greater** than the last 24 hours.

How we want things to be, and what God had planned for us to do, are sometimes at odds with each other. That's why we have to cling to something more than the daily events of the last 24 hours. Folks sometimes say, *it's not about this life, it's about the next*. Folks sometimes also interpret that to be that we should always try to do a better job of seeing God in every moment of the day. Other folks say, we better surrender to God and let him guide us through the day. The ultimate free will. Truth be told, the eternal outlook sure seems to be the secret to our contentment.

Because God has made Himself known to us ... we have full permission to lay our situations, pains, frustrations, disappointments and even despairs at His feet. As Ecclesiastes 3:1 tells us ..."*There is an appointed time for everything, and a time for every affair under the heavens."*(10) Trust God, to get us through the trials of life. That's was the plan, after all, from the start.

And y'know, in my sometimes upside down daily life, I'm OK with that. Trust, yeah.

... It's a good thing we've all got a past!...

I'm sure there will be a few folks shocked... but who we are, isn't the result of our superior ability to determine our own path, follow our own instincts, and relish our personal wisdom. Rather, who we are is the end product of a lot of good souls who impacted our lives and presented us with the templates of a fulfilled life ... good folk, in our lives.

Parents, Godparents and Grandparents – our role models, guardians and moral compasses ... our families and the seemingly infinite combinations of good intentions, reality checks, examples (pro and con) and support in times of joy, and times of testing ... Our teachers, from PreSchool through today, giving us abilities in reasoning, education and in making good and thought-through choices ... Our Clergy, religious and affiliates who weld our spiritual lives with the physical world for the good of all and the glory of God ... and those countless strangers we've all bumped into over our lives who in small ways, helped refine our character ... all contributing to who each of us has become.

And because of that past, and because of the countless folks who have had a hand in who we've become, we pray that, as we were created in the image of God, we are pleasing to God and are dependable vessels for the work He has for us to do in this life. May each and every one of us, gladly "pay it forward."

...So, where's the "do over" button?...

We take so much for granted, don't we? As if we got to where we are today by our own choices, sweat and pure determination on our part. Oh, God was there too ... but this is exactly where **we're** supposed to be, ... *'cause we chose the paths to follow to get here!* And then there's God's side of things ... that he gave each of us Free Will ... and **yes** he had a plan for each and every one of us, from before we were formed in the womb.

HE also gave us memory as His gift to us, and in that we can clearly recall the consequences of some of our choices. And once in a while we might wonder aloud why God let that happen when we wanted a different outcome ... y'know ... more time with Mom, that job that got away, peace and harmony in our family, fair weather friends? We knew what we wanted, why didn't God make it all work out right?

Well, God kind of got left out of those decisions. We may have chosen to be careless with our character, to be too harsh and unforgiving, spoken when we should have been quiet, making **big** lapses in judgment. And that's our human condition, and it's the default that kicks in when we choose to take what God wants, *out of our decision.* What's that quote ..."As ye sow, so shall ye reap."(11) And when we make bad choices, the devil howls in delight. And we lose heart. But that too is a choice, for in each and every trial and test God is always present, just waiting to be asked in. Don't give the devil his due, don't wish for a "do over" button, but DO surrender to God at this moment and His will for you and your soul, and He will in His way answer you, guide you and remain with you. As Jesus said ... ***Be it done unto Me, Father, according to Thy will.***"(12)

Michael Zibrun

...Being an example, being a fighter ... for life

Sometimes, in a person's passing, something still abides. The time for action is past, but the example of Life's priorities attend to our innate need to do good. Such are these thoughts, when we stand up in the 40 Days of Life ... Pro Life Movement. The site Priests for Life, published a number of quotes from Henry Hyde, Congressman from the state of Illinois, and a fighter for the unborn, facing that evil called abortion, and these His thoughts, seem to resonate in why protect life ...

*When the time comes – as it surely will, when we face that awesome moment, the final judgment, I've often thought as (Bishop) Fulton Sheen wrote, that "It is a terrible moment of loneliness. You have no advocates, you are alone, standing before God and a terror will rip through our soul like nothing you can imagine." But, **I really think** that those in the Pro Life movement will not be alone. I think there will be a chorus of voices that have never been heard in this life, but are heard beautifully in the next world and they will plead for everyone who has been in this movement. They will say to God, "Spare (him or her) because (he or she) loved us. And God will look at you and say not "Did you succeed?", but "Did you try?"*

Henry Hyde
1924 – 2007(12)

And check out the Priests for Life website, <u>Priestsforlife.org</u>. fer more good quotes from the late Mr. Hyde... a Great fighter for Life.

… your periodic performance review …

My goodness! Is it that time already? I thought I had more time before we take stock of where I am in life! Is there a Cliff Notes for the most likely to be asked questions?

What's the curve? I'm pretty busy now. UH … OOOH …

Well, every so often it's right to take stock of where we are in life, in how we are living our Faith practice and how we are managing to keep the bad side temptations at bay.

We were created by God in absolute love. We are to live in absolute love. And when the time comes, we will remain in absolute love.

So, maybe what we need is just a momentary reality check, eye to eye, in the mirror.

Are we in love with *our* Lord, *our* Savior, *our* Holy Spirit? Do we understand well, that how, we love Him, He loves us infinitely more. Do we do good things, in His name, and when he places those in need before us, do we also do good things in His name. Do we find it hard to tell where our pray life ends and the world's work begins, or does it all just, beautifully blend? Have we gotten better since when were three years old.. in our sharing with others, unconditionally? Oh, and saving the toughest question for last, ***Do we fully, unconditionally, and loving surrender to Him and His work for us, every day?***

So, I'll keep this brief. I'm off to do some mid course correction myself. Don't you wait, until **you've** got a hole in your schedule. Just like my grandsons in the Eagle Scouts, *Always Be Prepared.*

Michael Zibrun

... Does God really hear all our prayers? ...

It's surprising sometimes, when you talk with folks about things religious, and it seems as if there's a fair chunk of folks who haven't been asking for God's help for others, or for situations close to them. It's almost as if they may wait to bundle their prayers into on big prayer ... or maybe not even remember to pray to God. In those situations, they may have advice, they may have words of consolation, and even encouragement, but somehow the most important part of those moments are in the prayers that also could have been offered, and somehow weren't.

So, here's a few thoughts about prayers that might give us some guidelines. First, there is no size requirement of the things asked for though prayers. To God, every prayer is precious. Second, you don't have to worry about praying for the same thing, a lot, or maybe even every day. To God, every prayer is heard, every time it's prayed. Third, You don't have attach any terms and conditions to your prayers. God doesn't dance to our tune. He waits for prayers from the heart, not with deadlines attached.

I once read that ... ***when prayers are lifted up, it's as if Heaven is silenced for a moment so that He won't miss a word.*** That's a pretty comforting image, isn't it, when we may, in our fatigue, wonder if he's listening? Oh, yes He is. And His ability to hear each and every prayer, is infinitely greater than your prayers to Him. Trust in the Lord, for Heaven's – and your - sake!

…Simple is good … most always!…

There's an old song called *"Give me the simple life"*. And for many of us, right now, that sounds like a great idea, but it's probably not going to happen. A LOT of folks would be inclined to say …*"Hey walk a mile in my shoes and show me where simple is."*

But, just fer grins, what would simplicity *look like* if it surprised you and showed up on your doorstep? Would it immediately become your servant to tie up all those loose ends you can never get to? Would it be the ultimate organizer so that you would even have to think about a better "to do" list? Or would do a search for new ways to get more mileage from multi-tasking? Really?

Nah … Doesn't work that way. Simplicity, really, doesn't just show up. You, have to look for it. Simplicity does have its' own slogan. It goes like this …*"stop and smell the roses"*. And the one skill set we need to find it, is, in simply "observing." The enchanted moment when icicles coat a winter tree and the cold still air causes you to stop … and look. The aroma of a classic tea or special coffee. The soft smell of a baby fresh from a bath and smelling of lotion and shampoo. Clean sheets, or the luxury of reliving a happy thought, the moment from the past, when you felt Grace wash over you like a dry flood and Peace filled your soul.

These God moments bring order into the hectic moment, and sweet Simplicity follows. Sweet Simplicity is His promise too! A break in the day He's reserved for each and every one of us, not only for those of you who have it all together, but for also those of you who seem to have it all to do.

OOOOOPS! Can I get a Do-over?

Suppose, just suppose that you asked God about a "do-over" so you could have a better shot at *"getting it right"* in this life? Wouldja do it? " Hey no brainer! Oh yeah ... where do I sign? Yes, I believe in miracles! But, slow down the bus, Gus ... think it through carefully, before you leap for what you see as the Golden Ring. Or ya might be quotin' moreso "what a revoltin development this is."

Think first, about all those great and good happy moments that would now disappear. Think about your countless good deeds that have gone before you that now would be erased, forever. Think about an incalculable number of souls you prayed for that would be retracted and all the intercessions you've asked for yourself and other in this life, zero'd out. Y'know, some folks have a philosophy that it's not about this life, it's about the next life. Others believe that is where our treasure lies. Yet, This life, this one time, determines the next life. We may be reborn in Faith, but we're not reborn in body and soul ... until we get all the answers right.

Jesus made the very best of His 33 years on this earth. On the cross, he said "Father, let it be done to Me, according to Your will." Y'see, you got the Golden Ring when you were born! Among the good works you would do by your birth, began the first good work - the joy, love and wonder of your birth *by your parents*! Think about the Great, Good and Happy moments for others that would all disappear if you had a do-over ... every "pay it forward" moment that would forever not be paid ... every profession of Faith and Love you made to God which built up a huge storehouse of Grace in you, for you and through you to those you touched. ***GONE!***

Jesus came **one time** from the Father, for the salvation of souls. His legacy lies in the simple good deeds you do from the soul... the 1:1 conversation with a friend at the grocery store, being in right spot at the right time for someone in desperate straits, the spontaneous prayers for someone passing you in an ambulance, the strangers or friends who saw you do a good deed, and "got something from it."

Y'see in the end, it's not about our way, it's about His way in our lives. Always has been, even back to the Garden days. So, since ya have ta choose, choose His will, not your want, and be ever joy filled no matter what the hand life deals you. All we are guaranteed is that, all we really have is today ... make good choices and forget ... any regret.

...Why bother trying, in this goofy world anyhow?...

Y'know, sometimes you just want to pull the covers over your head and make it all go away. The nice thing about our town is that news coverage most always has more good news more than bad news. Yet so much of where we get our news seems to equate viewer, listenership, readership, or tweetership with the volume of bad news. What was the old adage from the 1960's ... _If it bleeds, it leads?_ Sometime it seems like there's not much good left to find, and we gotta be careful, _not to lose heart._ Was it much different, 2000 years or so ago?

So before, we get pulled into some dark places over all this, here's a couple o' picker uppers that might nourish us in the goofy times:

People are often unreasonable, illogical and self centered ... _be kind anyhow._

If you are successful, you will win some false friends and some true enemies ... _Succeed anyway._

If you are honest and frank, people may cheat on you ... _be honest and frank anyhow._

What you spend years building, someone could destroy overnight ... _build anyhow._

The Good that you do today will be forgotten tomorrow ... _do Good anyhow._

If you find serenity and joy, some may be jealous of you ... *Be Joy filled anyhow.*

Y'see in the final analysis, it's really between your "work in the fields", and God's plan to use you as His faithful servant. It was never about the naysayers, but maybe your example might change the hearts of, some day, the naysayers. . And remember above all else, God ... loves ... you.)))

…Here comes another ordinary week …

I think they call a lot of these days we have where nothing big, or special is really going on … *ordinary days.* Just a normal day in Adventure land. No great moments of clarity, no Walter Mitty dramatic rescues. No fawning adoration from the adoring public. Just another one foot in front of the other from early morning till end of day. Life is full of average days which don't really come up when you try to remember what happened two weeks ago.

And yet, I'll bet some really good things did happen two weeks ago, that we all might not consider a big deal in our week. Our standard response to the question at day's end of "How was your day?" is most always "OK", or "Nothing special", or "Fine" – which is code for "nothing special." Yet you did good in that day, and you did good not to be noticed, but because we are wired, mostly, to want to do good – however that happens.

You smiled at someone and they felt good. You had a kind word for someone and they appreciated your comment. You did something beyond what was expected and you never expected to be noticed for it. You said a prayer from the heart for someone else who would never know … and God heard it. Or, you chose not to get into a teardown fest of somebody's character because they don't have your point of view. Lots of moments … in that ordinary day. Grace is in those unremembered small moments – the ones unremembered by us but imprinted in ink in yer "book of your life" in eternity.

Mother Teresa said *"We cannot all do great things, but we all can do small things with great love."*(13) And, especially when life seems ho hum, take just a moment at days' end to say **"Thank you Jesus, for the** *folks you put in front of me that I was able to affirm, in however you used me to deliver that gift".* **Use me, as You see fit.**

Michael Zibrun

...For Heaven's Sake, Don't pull the thread!...

Imagine, for a moment, Our Lord weaving a most special blanket for each of us ... an infinite number of colored threads ... some seen by our eyes, some invisible, but all in one magnificent miraculous tapestry that drapes over our shoulder in this life. Imagine Him blending each thread correctly. Some threads of guidance, some of life's disappointments, some of sickness, some of great joy, and all infused with His boundless love for each and every one of us, and for everyone back to when time began.

The selection and the pattern is unique for each of us. No two are alike. And none of life's journeys are left out. Each strand infused with His eternal presence with us. Each strand, a reminder that we are never alone. Each strand an anchor that He walks with us and each strand a reminder that the Spirit is always there, simply waiting to be invited in. While the strands are already there, we determine through our openness, our free will and our surrender in life, how long each strand will be.

As our lives go on, He gently continues to weave the loosely fitting fringes tightly together with His loving grace. Sorrow, Sickness, Joy, Miraculous moments, Times of Great Fear, Contentment, Surrender and Countless number of other threads in that tapestry that He had planned for you, from before your birth. So this day, may His tapestry drape over your shoulders, shelter you and fortify you in wisdom.

And for Heaven's sake, **_Don't Pull the Threads!_**

... Plea Bargaining when
yer goin down ...

Well, here's a fine *how do you do,* moment. Just listening to Steve Tyrell's **In The Mood CD** on the Concord Music Group Label, and up pops a song I musta heard a hundred times and didn't connect the dots. So here's the connection. Steve's singin <u>*"I want a love that will last."*</u> (15) And, you can take that couple o' ways ... most always in a secular way. But Hey, this is a book about Timeless Advice, right? So whose more timeless than Jesus? Well, back up the bus, Gus and let's run over that at 33 1/3.

In all my years, I can't ever remember reading anything about Jesus singing. Now, I haven't read everything ... in fact I have a problem just getting thru some of it. But it stands to reason, that Mary must've taught Jesus some songs, right? And, wow, if <u>*Row, Row, Row your boat*</u> was one of them, does that speak *volumes* for the future, eh? I'm picturing Joseph joining in from the woodwork table.

Anyway, Cut five on Steve Tyrell's album talks about not wanting a memory ... how bein' 'here' when hopelessness tugs at your soul ... *whispering ..."Cash in yer chips, yer toast."* Hey, don't true love Win? Well, yeah, but ya gotta carry *yer cross ... truth be told, your burden is light, compared to HIS.* Did Jesus ask the same question? Nope. Jesus trusted in the Father. So don't talk like a potato. Close yer ears to the naysayers, and hold in your heart the truths that love wins, Faith will see you through anything, and Relationships ... can be forever. Check it out, Steve Tyrell, cut 5, on U-Tube.

...The New Models are out!...

Good News! ... if you're already beginning to think about the upcoming introduction of the New Models of Christian Faith fer next year! Basically, again there will be _no changes_ to our Models – as they remain the same as they have been over the last 2000-plus years (or waaaaaaaaay longer). This assures you of a countless number of examples to help drive your Faith life.

Our Faith history provides a countless number of Inspirational Faith Companions who have walked life's Peaks and Valley before us. For example, some folks find a kindred connection with St Francis of Assisi. A picture of him painted in words tells us that he was of cheerful countenance, of kindly aspect and his speech peaceable. He was said to be the more Holy of the Holy and among sinners was, as one of them.(16)

Y'know, you can select your own a Saint or Martyr as your constant spiritual companion to pray to, walking with you (so to speak) on your journey of life. Heavens! This life or the next, you can never have too many prayer partners! Those spiritual prayer companions also come with a 24/7/365 availability. So many of us are already blessed with great friends in this life. Well. Think about it. You've also got countless great friends in the next life too. All you have to do, is ... ask.

...Change o' seasons ...
Change o' reasons ...

Somehow, it sorta seems like we've moved from one season right into the next and didn't even have to pay a "toll" in jumping from one sport to another with the kids or grandkids.. But those of you with families sorta know the toll it took on you with soccer, baseball, gymnastics, football, tennis, hockey, scouts and a gazillion camps and tournaments to attend. And if your family is anything like mine, Free time (down time) is probably gonna be yer number one wish when ya pull together yer New Year resolutions at the end o' the year.

Holy Moley! Don't you just yearn for the days we used to read about of yesteryear, where multi-tasking in the old days was milkin' the cow and squirtin the kittens at the same time? How did this all get away from us? We had good intentions and wanted to do the right thing for the right reasons. But then, all those other things that snuck into our lives, really sorta pushed us and our dreams aside so that we almost have no time to think anymore. We're haunted by the things we can't get to because we're overloading on the things we have ta do. And, suddenly, we find ourselves unable to look ahead with excitement.

Good news from on high. God did not intend for you to become proficient in bi-location. Remember! He started out with a Garden of Paradise! He had no plans for highrises, activity centers or sports hubs. And, we all do what we gotta do. But WE, you or I, can decide where we invest our 24 hours in each day. May we choose, not in pressure, but in pleasure, that which brings joy, not obligation.

...Who wrote the "Book of Love?" ...

My sweetie, Carol Ann was a pre-school teacher whose passion in life was *"workin' with the babies"*. She used to say ..."If you want to know the truth ask a 4 year old." And she loved talking with them about Jesus,.. *always included the Good Book lessons*. And she always made sure that the stories were living stories, not dusty pass me downs. The Dress up extravaganzas at Christmas and the "flights to Hawaii" in her class were the stuff of legend. The Spirit of Love sure coursed through those stories.

It's a funny thing about reading stories ... and the best ones ever, especially in the Bible. Hey, smell the coffee! The Bible is the best Instruction Manual ever! Did you ever notice that once you've gone through an instruction manual, it's so often put aside, maybe packed away or simply filed in with the other 'rainy day stuff?" Sometimes the shelf life of the Instruction Manual can be for generations. It may look good up high on that shelf, maybe be a paperweight to hold up other books, and often, maybe packed away with a lot of other things. Sometimes, tragically, it's thrown away.

St. John Chrysostom once said ... <u>*The Scriptures were not given us, that we should enclose them in books, but that we should engrave them on our hearts".*</u> (15) What we often forget is that our **Biblical Instruction Manual** is also our **Maintenance Manual.** AHA! And that *engraving* process which is the heart of the Maintenance Manual is a living Testament that provides *24/7/365* for our souls for the length of our lives. And, those Good words ... those God words ... are to insure that our Faith life never goes out of Warranty- if we choose to follow the instructions.

Teacher had it right. And she and the babies would remember every time they sang along with the Angel Rabbit Gabriel … *Jesus loves me, yes I know, for the Bible tells me so … yes Jesus loves me … the Bible tells me so.*"

Michael Zibrun

"...Oh God of second chances ...
here I am again..."

We all have plans or dreams that push to reach new goals, improve ourselves or to fulfill a passion in our lives. Then, suddenly, something comes along and derails our quest. And, more often than not we find ourselves right back where we started. What happened, and where do we go from there?

Some say, *"Why can't we control of our lives? We have seen and learned how the world works, what rules the world plays by, and how behavior is rewarded. Therefore, we must know how to make the right choices! ... After all, that's why I have free will!"* Well, free will is also a dangerous temptress (or tempter) that may ignore the reality that God gave us free will to **also** choose to include Him life's decisions. Or not. When we don't, well ... consider Adam and Eve. God's plan was not to have it turn our as it did, but rather that we have a Heaven on Earth. But mans' and womans' selfishness and disobedience stained the gift God gave them, and us.

When times and circumstances turn our personal world and our plans upside down and inside out, it is precisely because God loves us so much, that those who turn to Him in times of testing find a way back from that dark place. *A second chance, if you will.* All we have to do is to completely surrender – no terms, no conditions. And in that act of truly believing *"Your way Lord, not mine"* **He will not abandon you**. He will help you to that place of second chances because He loves you. You are His great creation, and He does love you.

So, if life in some way suddenly takes a turn and you're out of options, *don't despair!* God gave folks like St. Peter and St. Paul second chances. All they had to do was to freely accept His way, and His will in their lives. And the rest – as they say – is history.

Michael Zibrun

...It's Always In The Eyes ...

Yikes! Are we running out of days of the year that can be called BLACK yet? Will we eventually just have a black month? I sure don't begrudge the shopkeepers in looking to bring in more customers. But I'm getting to feel guilty about the six places I miss in order to go to the two ... I did go to. What I'm *most* afraid of missing are the "hanging out with Jesus moments" I might trade away for the urgency I'm secularly pressured to act on. Let's not forget He IS, the reason for the season.

There's a great picture of Jesus you may have seen. It's called "*Hook's Smiling Christ*" and when you view it, it's as if His eyes are boring into yours ... eyeball to eyeball. Most Powerful! And over the years, I've come to picture that image ... His face six inches from my face ... 24 hours a day, seven days a week. Patiently, waiting to be invited in ..."Come to Me."(16) Check it out on the Web ... ChristCenteredMall.com

Our days are filled to overflowing with seemingly every distraction "Ol Scratch" can wing our way to keep us off balance, overloaded, frantic or obsessed with guilt even as the day draws near when we will celebrate the Anniversary of the Birth of Jesus. If we get sucked into that dark spot, we risk turning away from that face, those eyes and that sanctuary that will get us past the problems and the pressures crashing down around us, the hard times, the tears, the frustration, and yeah, even the helplessness. And here's His gift for those spiritual moments within the blackness when everything seems to be screaming at you ... **you just** need to invite Him in. Jesus, I trust in you.

...Do our days always include God?...

Interesting question, isn't it? Every morning we each face that choice. Do our first waking moments of the day begin with "**Good morning, God**"? In the first five minutes you're awake, what you do in those first five minutes sets the tone for how you are going to be throughout the whole day. If we immediately begin organizing for the dozens of things we want to have on our plate, well, that too will set the tone for the day. Our choice. The first five minutes you're awake sets the tempo and rhythm of our daily lives.

So why in the world is that so important? Well, why did God create us? He created us to know, to love and to serve Him. Remember that from first grade? To my knowledge, that applies in all 50 states, and for that matter, the rest of the world too. When we place God in the beginning of our daily lives, it opens us to letting Him in for the rest of our day. Remember, God doesn't force himself on us. We have to open the door and let him in. He is always there, simply waiting to be invited in.

Ya know what the difference is between an Optimist and a Pessimist? The Optimist wakes up in the morning and sez "Good Morning God!" The Pessimist wakes up in the morning and says "Good God, Morning!" God. God, first thing in the morning, through the day, and the last thought at night. It's really pretty simple. And, with all life may deal us, God also wants us to be happy too. We accept the daily crosses and we cherish His love for us. We do, control our day, when we let God in it with us. As a unknown writer once said, "God always has something for you, a key for every problem, a light for every shadow, a relief for every sorrow and a plan for every tomorrow." And it all starts with "Good Morning, God."

Michael Zibrun

..."Get out of Jail, Free" is a bad habit ...

... Came across an interesting little read the other day about **Loopholes** in our lives. It caused me to think about how we often – too often, really, add <u>wiggle room</u> to our responses when caught in our need to find a loop hole for "little white-lying" our way through an embarrassment moment. Y'see, it used to be *"the dog ate my paper"*, or *"I never got the message"*, then more recently, *"I had my phone on vibrate"*, or *"it must have gone into spam"*, or the<u> classic</u> ..."*I forgot I gave up meat on Fridays"*. And who could ever forget *"Flip? Flip who?"* from Christmas Story?

It's our human inclination, I think, to avoid looking less than perfect that makes our squirmy minds – or at least **mine** - LEAP in defense of anything that will start to tarnish this image we want others to have of us. Ol' Folk like me can cop a plea and say "Who are you again?" and thereby walk between the rain drops. But, our human condition is such that addressing the scandal of missing something, carries less weight than admitting our human condition. And, truth be told I think today's world, especially, we seem to embrace loopholes as part of our culture.

However, rest assured that as much as we would like others to believe we are perfect, the One who made us in His image, and which we have "secularly attempted to improve upon with time", well ..He sees **all**, remembers **all** and holds accountable ... **ALL** ... which brings us to Confession, where, fer us Catholics readin' this ... **ALL** ... can be forgiven. Little cracks in the asphalt become potholes that swallow small vehicles if left unchecked. Let's **all** admit our human condition and ... *Please, He who made us.*

...Is there ANY hope for this old world?...

Boy, it sure seems that a lot of people ... a lot of talking heads ... and a lot of really, really negative people nowadays seem quick to predict that the world is completely falling apart. It's all sounding now so hopeless and we're mislead by those thoughts, as powerless to change it You know, as difficult as life can be, HOPE and FAITH guide us and get us through these storms on the seas – these storms of life – this oft repeated cycle of history. But if you take away Hope and Faith, even the smallest of things can crush us.

The Bible tells us the true story of how God created us and our world, how WE fell away from his original design ... and what He did to heal our brokenness. Jesus died not when a whole lot of people were very, very good, He died when a whole lot of people were very, very bad... oh good folks amongst them, but bad actors all around. We are given the gifts of Hope and Faith to understand that God is in the business of restoring us to His beautiful intentions – if we let him.

Yet although God stamped His image in each and every one of us, SIN distorts that image And, if you listen to all the new age experts, we are being led into an "anything goes, no one is responsible mentality. The **true** reality is that our Hope and Faith rest on trusting God. Salvation has nothing to do with simply doing the minimums ... secularly obeying a set of roles or mechanically doing the right kind of good works or resigning yourself with just "going with the flow." Salvation comes from saying, from your soul ... ***Jesus, I trust in you.*** For when we authentically accept Jesus' terms for salvation, you can also trust that God will honor His agreement forever. Ironic, isn't it? It's when we surrender ... that we win!

Michael Zibrun

... the "art" of confusion ...

"Out of Order, comes Confusion" the better half once said about my perceptive powers of persuasion. I personally tend to wear with pride the reality that one of my core strengths is the innate ability to confound - and I gratefully wore that crown.

Funny thing is, I didn't get that crown new. It seems to have passed through a wealth of other folks and life situations capitalized on, at the expense of, well ... reason, logic, good manners, positive results, and happiness. Y'see, I don't think I actually invented something new. I think it was all around us. And, happiness, manners, good outcomes, reason and logic took an early 3 day weekend because of it.

Pick a direction. No matter which way we turn, we're slammed by the real "pros" who have known how to raise confusion to an Art form. I'd bet any one of us has a dozen sob-stories about things we participated in that promised great potential and fizzled 10 feet before the finish line. Buying Gold or Silver? Refinancing for the fourth time? Movin' on up to the East Side? Getting two dozen $1000 life insurance policies? Folks, its' all bananas.

Y'wanna talk treasure? Now, yer onta something. Let's talk about the treasures you'll amass in Heaven. Folks you've prayed for when they were deathly ill. Folks who left the world behind and went to their eternal reward. Kids prayed for with injuries. Young folks prayed for, for protection from temptations. Family members – even the snarky ones – who seem to be cryin' fer a shot of "good lovin" – spiritual kind. Folks ya don't like or even maybe hate, but prayin' for them nevertheless. Hey, we're all, still, children of God. And God don't make no junk, so we pray. That's where our treasure is.

The world will distract us, if we let it. So, turn yer back on the tempters of the world. Put yer hands together like a church steeple and just pray. May that confound the Father of Lies who may slink away to find easier *pickins* … and know yer Father, approves.

Michael Zibrun

...Don't stop now!...

Y'know, if you stop to take a deep breath, and try to slow down to find that inner peace we all long for, the odds-makers at the pony track are given3-2 odds you just might get there!

Yet that light at the "end of the tunnel" that gets all your vitals in the green-range again, isn't accidental. It's the culmination of all'o yer selfless acts, spontaneous help, and other appropriate actions yer mom or pop took ya to, long ago in yer early years.

When you and I were younger, it wasn't so much about amassing a ton of good deeds, it was just about doin' what yer heart and yer soul (and yer moms' voice in yer head) said was ... the right thing to do. We aint gonna know what kinda smile that brought to yer moms' heart muscle when she noticed it. But, right as rain, her pride in ya just went up a hundred notches – 'cause ya listened to good advice, and then did, good advice.

But, hey, it didn't then just dissolve like a selzer tablet. Y'see, yer good works linger. They always have. And, God loves that! They're the gifts that keep on given ... and, there's no expiration date either. Who knows what good thing you did, that picked up and multiplied into good works by others – y-know, pay it forward ... to help another soul in search of balance. Fer them, that's great!, Fer you it's just one more random act of kindness that polishes to a skuff-free brilliance, yer character. You are defined by who you love, and how you love. So, keep up the good work, y'hear?

A thought, on our daily struggles in life …

The missus and I really got hooked on a television series – back in the day – that I believe had a long and successful run on PBS called Anne of Green Gables. Lucy Maud Montgomery was the authoress, whose fictional writings were the basis for the books reprinted and the television series. The lead character, one Anne (with an e) Shirley was played by Megan Follows, whose orphan character was sent to Prince Edward Island in Nova Scotia, and the series followed her growing up with her reluctant "adopting parents."

The object of the attention was of course, orphaned "Anne Shirley", and she was portrayed as a young lady with an old soul, and the heart of a poet. And she continued to have, through the series, much to say about life, about its' challenges, and about the human spirit – on occasion. One such occasion presented itself which she expressed in these words … to the effect that, she felt *everyone has a book of Revelations within themselves.* (17) I chewed on that thought fer a while. And, y'know what? That makes a lot of sense.

Ya can't get yer arms around a Book like Revelations, 'till ya understand it was written as resistance literature to meet a crisis. For Gospel writer John, it was the persecution of the Church. For the ficticious Anne, it was her persecution as an orphan, not welcomed in society. Revelation tells us to stand fast in the face of adversity and God will triumph. And Ms. Montgomery's writings were pointing toward a waif, who chose not to go quietly, in the night. And, maybe that was the takeaway. Each of us, too, fights thru tests and trials, and holds onto the belief, that Good, will triumph. May we hold onto absolute trust that, in the end, "right" prevails.

Michael Zibrun

John's Book of Revelation is both an exhortation and an admonition to Christians of the first century to stand firm in the faith and to avoid compromise with paganism despite the threat of adversity and martyrdom. In the face of insufferable evil, either from within or without, Christians are called to trust in Jesus' promise ..."Behold, I am with you always."(18) No matter what adversity or sacrifice Christians may endure, we will in the end triumph over evil forces because of our belief in Christ our victor. Our imaginary Anne in the tale of Anne of Green Gables looks at her predicament thru the eyes of a child, and grabs a lifeline from the Good Book to help endure her own trials ... and comes to realize, that, *this* is the great human test all endure. Yet the end of the storm is always followed by the promise of a new day. For in Revelation 22:7, we read "Behold, I am coming soon."(19) Blest be the one who heeds the prophetic message.

...NEWS FLASH! ... Patient endurance trumps Jealousy...

It's pretty amazing how sometimes grown people find themselves in a jealous rage from social situations, workplace manipulation, errored Faith interpretations, perceived injustices or just plain mean spiritedness. Whew! And, they often get away with it too! I mean life is complicated enough without more unfounded stressors muckin' up the works.

It's like having a boat with rowers, rowin' in every direction ... 'ceptin' together. And the turf wars on that rowboat, incessant complaining, manipulative sabotage, gaming, judging, jurying and excutioning, all revolving around jealousy. I tell ya folks, it's all bananas.

After a lifetime o' livin, I've come to the conclusion that Jealousy seems to be a character trait as well as a huuuge flaw. And it often aint got a happy ending, does it? I don't think that it is part of God's plan ... I think I smell a snake in the grass. Sure we all have trials and tests, but in those tests – when old ugly rears his forked tongue head, God expects us to avoid slippin on the muck, step over the nuisance and keeping to that sweet narrow path.

I remember someone sharing with me once a conclusion he came to, long ago, that in life, ya got folks ya call yer friends, and ya got others that just seem to have it in, for you. He said *"there is no greater relief that the feeling you get when you forgive someone who had chosen to be your enemy ... and you choose to forgive them for that even though they'll never know it."* So I tried it, and it was true! 'See, it aint about revenge, it's about forgiveness, which carries one past the cheap shots, and desires for revenge, and in a faith model, extends mercy to those who may have lost their way a bit … or a lot. And with that, dear reader, for you comes Peace of Soul … as God had planned.

…Inspiration Now Available
in Convenient Sizes!…

Sometimes, we big folks need a "shot of inspiration" to help us through our days. There's a whole laundry list of places to get rejuvenated … talks, seminars, reading materials, DVD's, websites, certain authors who seem to touch our shoulder in compassion… in some way, seminars at the library or maybe kind words taken to heart from the pulpit, maybe side conversations with a friend, a special email and so much more.

But there's also an inspirational resource that tends to be overlooked … right in front of our eyes each day. They're called by various names, your child or children, your nephew or your niece, a teen ager, a young adult, a student, a daisy, cub or scout a wee one, or a baby. Do we comprehend at all, this great gift of children, from God, whom he may use to inspire us, to warm our hearts, to maybe just stop in simple awe, of the preciousness of life. Call an officials' time out when you find yourself in the graceful presence of the young ones. Inevitably, we get more from the experience than we give, and that's ok. Within our memories are treasures beyond compare. All for you, gentle reader …

To you, sometimes the small things in life may seem, bothersome or not worth a second thought. And yet, unbeknownst to you, the Good Lord may have planted little things right where you could see it, so you could hit the pause button … 'cause sometimes ya need to reset yerself. It's OK to hit the kill switch in that part o' yer brain that has ya thinkin' o' so much, ya get sorta paralyzed. Like now, with all these pages behind ya and still more to come. It's ok to stop. Soak up the silence, let yerself just drift a bit. Amazing how nice silence sounds … when ya just hit the "pause" button.

Michael Zibrun

...The oft-told tale of the ol' log cabin in the woods ...

A gentle soul was sleeping in a cabin, when suddenly the room filled with light and God appeared! The Lord said he had work for that person to do, and showed a large rock that was in front of the cabin. The Lord said "I want you to push against that rock with all your might, every day. And so the person did so, day after day. For many years, from sunup to sundown the person toiled with every bit of strength - shoulders set square against the cold, massive surface of the unmoving rock ... that souls pushed will all the might available, yet there was no movement. It seemed the effort was in vain.

Since that soul began showing discouragement – the ultimate adversary, ol scratch, decided to enter the picture by placing discouraging thoughts into the person's head." *"Hey, enough is enough. You pushed a long time and nothing gave. So what gives? You're a failure, you always will be. Admit it."* And that poor soul began to lose heart. But, in the end, the good soul decided to turn it back to God.

And God said, "my friend, when I asked you to serve me, you did, and I told you your task was to push with all your might. You did. Never once did I mention I wanted you to move it. Your task was to push. And in the process, your muscles grew strong, hands callused and arms and legs toned and hardened for good works and deeds to come. My call was to be obedient, and to exercise your faith and trust in my Wisdom. You did. So, Now, I will move it.

God wants us to exercise Faith that will move mountains. Yet know, it is God who will move those mountains. He needs YOU to PUSH *"Pray Until Something Happens!"* When things go south, money, job, friendships, bills, pressures … just PUSH!

…Danger … soft shoulder ahead …

A Pal o' mine from the old days and myself worked together at a big ol' company for a while up north o' Chicago. Mark Madsen was a guy who did the business gig deal during the, day, and then spent the nights and weekends singing solo or with the City Lights – croonin some o' the really great standards of the old days. In particular, I was always taken with his spin on a tune called **DETOUR AHEAD.** (20) It's a song about a defining moment of Love, or Love lost. And, it points to the fragility of making a life changing decision, or not. Check Mark and his music out on <u>markmadsenworld.com</u>, you'll be hooked!

So, I told ya that, ta tell ya this. I still remember my mom telling me that the road to paradise in Heaven, forever, is a real narrow path. And if yer not careful, it's real easy to slip off that path and wind up stuck forever at the bottom of that slippery slope. And because we all have this thing called Free Will, we make our choices that either bounce us back to the center o' that path, or derail us quicker than Casey Jones train wreck in ol Steam Engine '99.

Y'see God intended that, that path to Eternal Salvation was a pretty straight shot. All Adam and Eve had to do was to stay on the path and all good would be good, forever. But poor decision making took em over the cliff before you could say "Wadda doin? Did you just fall of the Turnip truck?" And the rest is History.

I think that when that path was placed before each of us, God also planted on both sides of that path ... *plants of grace ... so we could grab something!, that'd keep us from doin' a half gainer off the cliff.* All we gotta do is Trust, and He will provide the hope to cling to, to keep us from that headlong half gainer. One might succumb to the temptations and abandon Him, but He'll never abandon us. Ever.

...A potpourri of, well, words ...
that I wrote, or found ...
that got me through ...

Trust God, who loves you more than you love yourself, to always bring about what is best for you. (u-no-who)

"Don't ask what the world needs. Ask instead what makes you come alive, and then go and do it.. Because what the world needs are people who come alive. (David Steindl-Rast: Common Sense Spirituality Crossroad 2008)

Stay in the present moment! The past is over, the future doesn't exist yet. Here and now, THIS moment in time, is all you have.

What makes you come alive? What is your deepest desire? Find it! Follow it!
Say what you mean. Don't talk against yourself or gossip about others. Use the power, THE POWER of your words for truth and love.

YOU are somebody's role model!

Don't take anything personally. What others say and/or do isn't about you. It's about them. Don't worry about the opinions or actions of others.

(my favorite) Do not go, where the path may lead. Go, instead, where there is no path, and ... *leave a trail! (*Ralph Waldo Emerson)

Don't make assumptions. Find the courage to ask questions and express what you really want to avoid having misunderstood.

"You must **be** the change you wish to see, in the world" (Mohammed Ghandi)

Hey, Always do your best. God didn't make you, average. He made you in His image. *Think of that for a moment!* God don't make no junk.

...Does God, weep?...

Have you ever given much thought to wondering if GOD weeps? Look at everything from the Garden at first to the Gazillions of inhabitants at present. Remember, what ever that Ginormous number must be, that each and every one was formed by God in the image and likeness of God. And each one, formed in the womb to be born of the womb, was born to know, love and honor God. So, how is humanity doing ... in its' attention to purpose?

Imagine, my brother or sister reading this, if you and I could see what God saw when he created all this! And imagine the painful impact made on him of others' choices, made for selfish advantage, not for His kingdom building. Every single thing you or I do, or think, or choose will impact on the one who created you. Imagine throughout all of history, the babies that were never born, the elderly who were cast aside like driftwood, the folks most in need for life saving help, never receiving it for that assistance was deemed not for the common good.

In truth, all we really have is today. So, with this day, given you by God, invest wisely. May all you do today bring Him joy, and may your words, thoughts and actions today please him and help others today, and every day for the rest of your life.

...A Reading Of An Offering
Of The Self...

"O LORD

MAY MY SOUL BE FLOODED WITH YOUR LIGHT

AND KNOW YOU MORE AND MORE PROFOUNDLY!

LORD, GIVE ME SO MUCH LOVE,

LOVE FOREVER, SERENE AND GENEROUS,

THAT I WILL BE UNITED WITH YOU ALWAYS

LORD,

LET ME SERVE YOU AND SERVE YOU WELL,

ON THE PATHWAYS THAT YOU WISH OPEN TO ME

AND TO MY EXISTANCE HERE, BELOW."

POPE JOHN PAUL ll

...Daydreaming was
invented by God too!...

Set your own pace. When you're pushed, let folks know they're pushin'

Taking nothing for granted. Watch water flow, walkers walking, sunsets

Quit planning ever detail. God's in control

Taste your food. He made it for you, to delight and nourish

Play with children, it brings out the child in you ... *I told you so!*

Stand outside, and just listen to the wind blow

Give yourself permission to be late, not permission to beat yourself up

Watch and listen to the night sky ... it speaks to you

Whatever your age, make time for play, it keeps you young

Grab a paragraph out of the bible daily, it's spiritual vitamins

Listen to the language of a bird, singing

Pray spontaneously, when ya feel like it, when ya don't

(you'll love this!) Take time to be lazy, sleepy or unproductive

Talk slower, life ain't Instagrams

Have a spot in yer home that's your own little hermitage

Fergive yerself if ya mess up, and laugh about it later

Always make sure to ask God for what you need, then wait

Listen to all yer families' stories … they are, your legacy

Smile, always, even if ya don't want to

… and, gentle reader … make every minute count.

...When Life deals ya a busted flush ...

O Lord

Help me to live this year ... quietly, aaand, easily

To lean upon your great strength, Trustfully, restfully

To wait for the unfolding of yer will, Patiently, serenely

To meet others, Peacefully, joyfully

To face each tomorrow courageously

<u>*Don't ever*</u> *let go of my hand*

…Ya got yer dance card filled out yet?…

In the old days, of the last century, shortly after dirt had been invented, Our 7th Grade dance class at Divine Infant Jesus Grade School had assembled for a major announcement from Miss Crimmons, our Dance Instructor. Miss Crimmons was the only instructor (male or female) who's medium of instruction was castanets. After clicking vociferously, she announce that we would be preparing for our first formal 7th grade class dance. And she was to expose us to the art of several different styles of dancing.

And so, we found ourselves, acquiring rudimentary movements which occasionally coincided with recognized dance styles. We learned the waltz, the box step, the shuffle ball chain (which would be a life saver when the Stroll would be invented five years later) a stab at a foxtrot… and the Polka, *which personally always whipped me into a frenzy.*

Aiding 30 7th graders in dance techniques was akin to herding cats. But, most all got some semblance of more formal dance. She then proceeded to give each of us a blank dance card and a golf pencil. We were to write partners for dances on the card for next week's dance. I wrote Pat McCarthy's name and put ditto marks all the way down 'cause she was a pretty good dancer. And, other than a few who seemed to trip consistently, it went well. Now, I told ya that, to tell ya this.

Life calls you and I to work on our dance cards too. Some of the circle of friends and family we have, seem to be doin' ok and their cards seem full. Others, have holes that need to be filled and nobody is steppin forward. Others we hardly ever hear about because of distance or obligations on our part. Maybe it's time to dust off that dance card, and see who needs a partner today. Maybe some of you remember when no one asked you to dance. Be there for them.

Michael Zibrun

... Look both ways!...

Our moms' advice growing up was always worth listening to, wasn't it? And more times than not, the Frank Sinatra thing doing it "my way" always seems fraught with painful consequences that helped us to discover that virtue called "humility." And more times than not, Dads' response was <u>don't do it again</u>, and Moms' was <u>Well, what did you learn</u>?

"Look both ways" is one such example that seems to have gone out of fashion, in a goofy world that advertises to "*just do it*", or "*click here*" or "*don't wait, act now, operators are standing by* – somewhere in the world, eh? The world has tried to move us to Warp 9 so that "thinking" gets thrown out with the weekend papers, and the new truth is that it's moving pretty fast, and like Ferris Bueller, "*if you don't hop on, you're gonna miss that great ride! ... cause things are spinnin' pretty fast.*" And there's a lot of truth in that last part. The intensity of life, seems to be like that ride they used to have at Riverview Amusement Park in Chicago, Illinois–THE ROTOR – where you were helpless plastered on the walls of a revolving drum like **sealcoating**. What a way to live life, right?

That's not what God intended. Jesus was always pointing out that life was choices, and his constant prayers, public speaking and messages through his disciples, followers and hidden supporters, was "*choose wisely, and be better for it*". "Look both ways in those times was to say, Look to the right ... and look to the wrong." We're in control of our souls, and we can choose acceptance of his love and direction, or we can go solo and follow the words and music of that hit "my way" song from yesteryear and launch into the deep with spiritual lead weights on our ankles.

One of the innumerable great things about God, tho, is that He don't abandon you when ya choose to launch of instead of lookin' both ways first. He's still there, waitin' fer ya to say sorry as ya getting' that sinking feeling … and always extending a hand to lift you when ego or instant gratification gets put back into its' proper place and common sense gets back on your personal hit parade. So, whom shall we listen to, today?

Michael Zibrun

... Getting Charity Exposure
Syndrome Yet?

Boy, there sure are a wealth of Charities of all types and stripes mailing us for aid and support for the work they do, the folks they help, and the impact charity has on so many of those good folks in need. And, I must confess, when I receive a mailing with anniversary cards, get well cards or work gloves! (fer some reason), pens, church cards, keychains, and a plethora of wearable or useable items in sometimes "kinda big" bags, I wonder what their cost is to send out sweeteners, versus if they just sent the request will a real nice letter that explained to good they do, and how, perhaps a donation might extend their reach of good works? I just came back from checkin' fer mail at my curbside mailbox and I swear I heard the box chokin' on a postal hairball.

Yeah, we all got our own charities that we keep goin' back to, that nobody else knows about. And we do don't do it fer bragging..ie: *"save the seaslugs"* ... *but fer a bunch o' good causes.* I'm just fearful we're gonna have a Black Guilt Day someday, fer the ones we missed ... livin' with regret while I watch my Kohls' card smolder, as I peruse the $10 and under, guys' racks for the guys in a hard place.

So here's the deal. Instead of me havin' ta wear another hat o' judge and jury, why don't I let the Big Guy touch my heart fer the ones, that He may have assigned to me. Who better to turn to for waste not, want not, eh? It sure is better than feelin' guilty where it shouldn't be. And, if ya need a pair o' gloves, I may be able to *help ya.*

...The Center is most always the playmaker ...

Back in the day before they had a big "clothes horn" that today comes over you and plasters every inch of yer kid in equipment, pads, a garter belt fer yer socks, gloves, helmet, skates and sticks, there was **Gunzo's**. **Gunzo** was a former goalie who did a tour with the Chicago Blackhawks and stayed in Chicago and ran a Hockey store ... sorta like a Hockey Store to the wannabe stars. And Stan Mikita, ol' 21 on the Hawks, was my hero! Still got his stick! And life, was good!

Yer's truly was once upon'a time a Hockey Player fer Elmhurst College in Elmhurst Ill.. And a Center, to boot! Why, we even had Canadians on the team, and winger named Bill who was a 50 goal scorer one season. I had started out as an 11 year old with toilet paper tucked into the skate toes 'cause my brothers skates were waaay too big ... on a man-made pond courtesy o' the local fire department folks ... played in High School and then with the Elmhurst "Eagles" (our name fer our team since Blue Jays was the official team name fer the other sports). I would never be really good at Hockey, 'cause I missed all the basic stuff of earlier years. But it sure was fun. Y'see the Center tends to often be the playmaker ... settin' up folks fer a shot at glory and a goal.

Now, I wrote that, to say this ... I think, in life, each of us is "charged" in some way, bein' a center for others. How many times in yer life, gentle reader, have you set someone up to have a clear shot at a goal. How many times have you blocked out trouble around someone who just needs to be "open", fer a change? How many times did ya get somethin' to someone who wasn't expecting it, and they did good with it? How often did ya let someone have a moment to bask in a personal

Michael Zibrun

best, 'cause you fed him (or her) what was needed to score. And the crowd went wild! ... er at least happy! May we all be surrounded by teammates in life (including the best coach ever from on High), who truly care, and does bring out the best ... in others if we follow His instructions.

...Y'can teach an old geezer new tricks! ...

As ya get older, one of the things that happens is that it's easy to remember all the good times, and even easier to forget the lame brain stuff that took ya down a path that wasn't the yellow brick road. So, bein' a standup guy, It seems right to draw on a life of choices and share a couple o' nuggets earned the old fashioned way. sooooooooooo ...

I've learned that the best classroom in the world is at the feet of an elderly person.

That, when yer in love, it shows.

That no matter how serious life is, everyone needs a friend to act goofy with.

That, since even God didn't do it all in one day, what makes you think you can?

I've learned that when ya plan to get even with someone, you only wind up letting that person continue to hurt ya.

That one should keep one's words soft and tender in case ya gotta eat 'em later.

That a smile is the best way to improve yer looks.

I've learned that to ignore the facts, does not change, the facts.

Michael Zibrun

That we should be really, really thankful God doesn't give us everything we ask for.

That under that hard shell, is someone who just wants to be loved too.

That Children are, the greatest of blessings one can have in life.

That nothin is sweeter than fallin' asleep with yer baby's or grandbabies breath on yer cheek.

That love, not time, heals all wounds.

That I sure didn't deserve the Lady I married, yet I have been, truly, the luckiest man in the world. May you also relish yer good fortunes, too.

An my personal favorite ... *the less time I have to work with, the more I get done.*
Go figure!

...Is the big blue marble
spinnin' a bit faster?...

Now, folks, I haven't personally seen any farm animals bein' flung into space, one must admit that we seem to have lost some of our control of the days, the weather, the obligations and master blueprint locked into our brain for getting stuff done! And an hour is still an hour, a minute still a minute, but somehow the margins are movin' toward the center and life is getting' compressed. We got all that fancy gadgetry to alarm our day for efficient use of time, but y'know what? The satisfaction is missing! Y'know, savoring that aftertaste in our souls that come with the moment of accomplishment.

Each day becomes like a tick mark on a calendar. How come the kids get it, how to get through the day … as a kid! And here we are, tryin' to keep the 15 plates spinnin round and round, and not havin' any o'them fall off the balance sticks while the music blares out the notes to the Sabre Dance? Where did our childhood go to?

So here's a thought or two that might be worth chewin' on, a bit. How about turnin' yer back on that hornets' nest, and just go off the grid? How about stepping away in yer mind and soul, and just … go quiet … and just wait? You see, it's important to understand that when you choose to wait, you are really taking action. You can't become whatever next God wants you to be, if your distracted by the churn of everyday distractions. So, when you get to this break point, well … break with all that distraction and go quiet. Wait for whatever next God has planned, and have no fear. He will lead you in ways you can't imagine to something much greater. All ya have to do, is wait!

Michael Zibrun

...Getting on the same page, as ... Him...

OK, so waddathink? Does try'in to believe and trust that Jesus really will overturn the hopelessness we're assaulted with in a world gone somewhat batty? A lot o' people are tryin' real hard to convince us that most everything in the world is our of your or my control. And, it may get even uglier. Y'now, if ya let it, them incessant carpet bombing updates on a world gone wild. Accidents. Shootings. Recent Polling that attacks our heart and will, and if we're not careful, buries our resolve.

When ya accept something as being true, it changes what you do, how you feel, and where you can make a difference, or ... change an outcome ... or find REAL balance. Y'see Christ is real, you accept that ... and, you trust. Our salvation doesn't come like earning enough points to get a "D-" (its still passing, right?), but rather not tryin to 'game' the system, and instead spending each day, really, in love with Him. Mary and Joseph understood that! So did the Apostles, and all those from then to now who believed in Him Really, believed in Him

Salvation is God's gift to you and me. We own that. Our issue is to make sure we hold onto it, and don't lose it. No matter how badly you might be damaged, no matter how many awful choices you may have made, - even up to rejecting God - Jesus can forgive you. But you gotta get on the same page as Him. It is, your choice. So, turn it over to Him. Confess, your desire to be in His grace. Hey, that's why it's called a Leap of Faith. Just do it! He'll catch ya!

...Unreasonable People ...

Your strength is in doing what is right
And not concerning yourself with
other people's responses

Unreasonable people gain their power
from the way you react to them

Children tease other children not because they are evil
but because they feel powerless

All unreasonable people you meet gain power
From your response

When you respond emotionally
You give them victory

How do you manage unreasonable people?

You dismiss them
Like teasing, like shadows

Michael Zibrun

...So, who can ya trust, nowadays?...

Us dinosaurs remember, times past, when our trust was in folks like the late Walter Cronkite, the late Huntley-Brinkley team Nightly new and Chicago's locally home grown, newscaster Fahey Flynn and old ol' reliable weatherman Clint Yule. These guys gave us the straight skinny with no grandstanding included. Words like integrity, character and trust. Well, that slate got washed pretty clean in the ensuing decades, and what was once trust has now morphed into - for better or worse - the likes of facebook, and the internet, dolled up personalities in expensive garb. *Poor ol' Mike Royco, Page 2 writer from the old Chicago Sun Times* gotta be spinning like a top, at all the changes to his craft. Truth is morphing into who yells the loudest. Integrity is confused with ratings.

I think a lot of us, miss, the old days.

So, getting' a bit preachy, the Apostles faced the same situation when Christ died on the cross. They gathered in prayer, but Jesus was not in their midst. And the world was preparing itself to take care of those 11upstarts and their followers. And while Jesus prayed for ones the Father has given him, He knew that all whom He loves to the ends of the earth, are redeemable, if they trust Him. I daresay, trusting, unconditionally, may be the hardest thing to do. You put 100% of yourself out there, as Jesus did. But at the same time, you and I know the snake in grass is tryin' to worm his way into our acceptance. So, here's the exception to the rule. Pay no heed to the one whose medium is dirt, and dismiss him, like a wave of a hand. Trust in Jesus, is eternal.

Luke Warm isn't just a cowboy hero ...

When each of us, starts our new day, some of us may have that "wish list" or "to do" list for the day, already prepared the night before. And, as they say, when you hit the door runnin, you really are: time management, consolidation of trips, power dialing, to do lists, obligations you can't cancel ... and a whole bunch more clawin' at ya and daring you to miss doing one, so you can end your day with guilt feelings. Others may reject the placing of many monkeys on one's back and just "wing it" which often ends in guilt over failure to launch. We always obsess on the one, we missed, don't we?

Either way, yer calendar's full of impositions that need getting' done or a laundry list of wishes ... and odds are, yer' gonna miss some and then get haunted by guilt. Y'know, the old expression ... *Hey! There are only so many hours in a day?* Many times your first hour or so that yer awake, sadly don't include the whole Prayer side of things. In fact, the only time prayer may start yer day, is when you find yourself backed up in traffic and you invoke the Almighty ... ***Aw good Lord, wouldja just look at that! ...***

Society, in general, ain't about life with a faith foundation. And given the demands on each of us, our Faith anchor is more like a Hills Brothers 16 ounce coffee can with pebbles in it, than it is the great balancer of daily life... Luke Warm, at best, given that busy life is the new normal. And, truth is, God don't do no Luke Warm. God is an all-in God. We nip around the edges of that, mostly. It's sorta like *Secular* is workin' real hard to be the new norm. And in our business, that may become our default mode. Luke Warm is "Yup, I'll follow you, just let me go bury my father first." Followed probably by a bunch more of delays and deferrals. Faith first, brothers and sisters ... Faith thru each day Faith for those spontaneous moments in the day. Feed your Faith first, and your doubts and hesitations and wrong choices will starve to death.

...Yesterday, Today, Tomorrow...

There are two days in every week about which we should not worry … two days which should be kept free from fear and apprehension.

One of these days is Yesterday, with its' mistakes and cares, its' faults and its' blinders, its' aches and pains. Yesterday has passed forever beyond our control.

All the money in the world cannot bring back Yesterday. We cannot undo a single act we performed. We cannot erase a single word said. Yesterday is gone.

The other day we should not worry about is Tomorrow with its' possible adversities, its' burdens, its' large promise and poor performance. Tomorrow is also beyond our control.

Tomorrow's sun will rise, either in splendor or behind a mast of clouds … but it will rise. Until it does, we have no stake in Tomorrow, for it is yet unborn.

This leaves only one day, Today. Anyone can fight the battles of just one day; It is only when you or I add the burdens of those two awful eternities – Yesterday – and Tomorrow – that we break down.

Michael Zibrun

It is not the experience of Today that drives us mad – it is bitterness or remorse for something that happened Yesterday and the dread of what Tomorrow will bring.

Therefore, Let us live but one day at a time.

"Yesterday is a cancelled check, tomorrow is a promissory note. Today is ready cash. Spend wisely"

..."Have I Told You Lately
That I Love You"...

Have I told you there's no one else above you
Fill my heart with gladness, Take away all my sadness
Ease my troubles that's what you do ..."

This little snippet was something I stumbled across a hundred years ago. I was running a series of simple sessions on getting through the rough patches when life wants to keep ya paralyzed. I called it *"my Cross"* 'cause folks figured it was just their cross to bear. Over time, and affirmations, and mutual support and an occasional tune to peek around the corner and find inner strength waiting, and the sessions concluded with a bit more clarity on getting past the rough time. There were a few songs that helped along the way, including the one mentioned above. It, simply, said it all.

That one, really touched heartstrings. Curious? Check it out, listen to it, then go back again and *really listen* to it.

Sung by Rod Stewart
Released June, 1993
Lyrics by Van Morrison
Sony/ATV Music Publisher
Check it out on UTube 11,528,758 hits

Michael Zibrun

...A Tribute to my Gramma Carol...

By Hailey Loyd

My Gramma was so tough and strong

She could have probably beat King Kong

She was so caring, loving and sweet

My Gramma always liked to cook up a treat

She's the person to pick you up from a fall

She'd always love taking trips to the Mall

My Grandmother passed away in 2011

So, I guess I'll see her in Heaven

I love my Grandma

"Let the little children come to me and do not hinder them. It is to just such as these, that the Kingdom of God belongs. I assure you that whoever does not accept the Kingdom of God as a little child, shall not enter into it. Matthew 19:14-15

…It has been so very nice, to have this time together …

And so, gentle reader, as we draw to a close, I hope the following lines from special people, in some way stay with you. As Jesus said "take heart, <u>I have conquered the world.</u>' May you find Peace and Renewal …*and, don't forget to smile.*

Michael Zibrun

...Sacred thoughts...

God does not die on the day when we cease to believe in a personal diety, but we die on the days when our lives cease to be illumined by the steady radiance, renewed daily, of a wonder, the source of which is beyond all reason
Dag Hammarskjold General Secretary UN MARKINGS

I once spoke to my friend, an old squirrel about the Sacraments – he got so excited and ran into a hollow in his tree and came back holding some acorns, an owl feather, and a ribbon he had found. And I just smiled and said "Yes, dear, you understand ; everything imparts His grace.
St. Francis of Assisi, from his writings edited by Daniel Ladinsky in Love Poems from God

We may ignore, but we can nowhere evade the presence of God. The world is crowded with Him. He walks everywhere incognito. And the incognito is not always hard to penetrate. The real labor is to remember, to attend. In fact, to come awake. Still more, to remain awake
C.S.Lewis *Letters to Malcolm*

Whoever has a desire to keep his life safe, will have it taken from him; But whoever gives up his life because of me, will have it given back to him
Jesus – the Gospel of Matthew

There are only two ways to live your life. One is as though nothing is a miracle. The other is as though everything is a miracle.
Albert Einstein.

The great lesson from true mystics ... is that the sacred is in the ordinary, that it is to be found in one's daily life, in one's neighbors, friends and family, in one's back yard.
Abraham Maslow The Farther Reaches of Human Nature

Index of Footnote References

(1) Psalm 23 Book of Psalms Catholic Study Bible (CSB): New American Bible

(2) Jeremiah 1:5 CSB New American Bible

(3) 1 Peter 2:24 CSB New American Bible

(4) Genesis 1:9 CSB New American Bible

(5) Luke 8:24 CSB New American Bible

(6) St. Francis De Sales Essential Wisdom of the Saints Carol Kelly-Gangi (2008)

(7) Hostatio: Sam Ewing Brainyquotes.com

(8) Luke: 9:59 CSB New American Bible

(9) Ecclesiastes 3: CSB New American Bible

(10) Galatians 6:7-8 CSB New American Bible

(11) Luke 1:38 CSB New American Bible

(12) A New Standard: Give me the simple Life Steve Tyrell Atlantic Records (1999)

(13) Luke 22:42 CSB New American Bible

(14) Mother Theresa ChristianQuotes.com

(15) Steve Tyrell "I'll Take Romance" CD Concord Music Group Cut 8 2012

(16) St. John Chrysostom Pinterest.com

(17) John 7:37 CSB New American Bible

(18) L.M. Montgomery Journals 1913 Anne of Green Gables

"Sometimes Scripture can be a challenge to understand exactly how it can be used in daily life. This is when Mike Zibrun steps in and makes it perfectly clear with homespun and sage advice, with just the right amount of humor ... like a bow on a much appreciated gift."

Antonietta Nicklaus

"Mike's columns are filled with wit, wisdom, joy and love. In his unique homespun style, he guides us deeper into our Faith and closer to God, while always filling our minds and hearts with "food" for the journey

Greg D'Anna

Mike's business career spanned over 45 years and his preferred mediums were in advertising, marketing and customer service. For over 2 decades, he headed S. Michael Associates,. He's authored 3 industry books. He lives in Sycamore Illinois and is a member of St. Mary Catholic Church in Sycamore Illinois. He can be reached at TimelessAdvice@gmail.com.

Printed in the United States
By Bookmasters